Far Out Isn't Far Enough

Gull's eye view of place on high tide

Tomi Ungerer

Far Out Isn't Far Enough

Grove Press, Inc., New York

First Hardcover Edition 1984
First Printing 1984
ISBN: 0-394-53878-1
Library of Congress Catalog Card Number: 83-49425

First Evergreen Edition
First Printing 1984
ISBN: 0-394-62189-1
Library of Congress Catalog Card Number: 83-49425

Printed in Great Britain

GROVE PRESS, INC., 196 West Houston Street, New York, N.Y. 10014

*With acknowledgement
to my friend Burton Pike
for his editorial support.*

British Library Cataloguing in Publication Data

Ungerer, Tomi
    Far out isn't far enough.
    1. Farm life – Nova Scotia
    I. Title   II. Heute hier, morgen fort.
    English
    971.6   S522.C2

    ISBN 0-413-55630-1 (hardback)
         0-413-54580-6 (paperback)

Hell is the devil's paradise.

This book is dedicated to my wife Yvonne (and to myself).

Yvonne and I left New York City in 1971, head over wheels. We were suddenly fed up with city life: racing along, our lives had run out of fuel, stalled, and so we struck out on foot on the first side road, not even expecting the unexpected.

Six months before we left New York we had gone to Nova Scotia on a holiday. There we had found a wrecked house and bought it as a future vacation spot. It stood on a peninsula; two sand beaches joined it to the wooded mainland. A pond lay caught between the beaches. At the tip of the peninsula was an island which could be reached only at low tide. To get to our property you had to wait for low tide and then drive across the beach on the hard surface of fine white sand. The nearest town was two miles away.

It was only three years later that we had a road built through the woods.

The town, Gull Harbor, with a population of some two thousand souls, has a harbor which at the time we moved there counted three large fisheries. Fish, lobster and scallops are the only source of income. But the town is a far cry from what it used to be: in the old days it prided itself on three boatyards, a foundry famous for its cooking stoves, three hotels, and a sawmill with a dance hall on top of it.

The town has no bars, but a state-run liquor shop. Nine brands of religion divide the population. Pentecostals, Baptists, and Jehovah's Witnesses to mention just a few. There used to be a Catholic church which was turned into a library. These religious denominations seem to agree on one thing: the evils of alcohol. It is forbidden by law to drink outside your home. Most wives seem to support this law. So what does the rum-starved fisherman do when he comes ashore . . . ? Hide and drink. The effects of clandestinity exacerbate the effects of drink, and that spells trouble. There are no local police; the last town cop was beaten up and gave up his job. The Mounties stationed in Newbridge, the county seat some eighteen miles away, pay occasional visits. This does not suffice to reinforce either law or order in a society where guns can be bought at the grocery store and where people go deer hunting sporting Lee Enfields from the Second World War. More recently, the use of drugs instead of liquor may have reduced some of the violence, but this is only speculation.

The great majority of the population does not get drunk and lives in God-fearing unobtrusiveness. Liquor or not, you will find people pleasant, hospitable, and very helpful . . . .

When we made our move our house had already been partially repaired. There was electricity, running water pumped from the well, and a toilet emptying into a sceptic's tank.

We arrived with our two Burmese cats, Piper and Heidsieck, and soon afterwards acquired our Newfoundland dog, Sacha. We settled upstairs on a mattress between two piles of lumber. Our furniture and miscellaneous belongings remained in storage for a long while.

We had no idea what to expect. We had not planned to establish a homestead, start a farm, or anything like that: the return to Mother Earth was not so much in fashion then. We were more like refugees, not knowing why or from what.

It was after our first visit to the butcher that we decided to raise some of our own meat. I had bought a chicken and simply asked him to piece it out . . . . To my dismay he sliced the beast with his band saw (the chicken was not alive) and handed it back to me like a set of books, the fleshy equivalent of my six volumes of Gibbon's *Decline and Fall of the Roman Empire* . . . . A whole side of veal met with a similar fate. This gave us the incentive to become our own butchers.

Our place was surrounded with good grazing, so we started some sheep. Our first sheep was called Tippy because the tip of one ear was black. The second one was named Flitter. We liked them, we killed them, we ate them.

They were the first animals, followed by many others: chickens, ducks, geese, rabbits, goats, cows, pigs, horses. We even tried to raise wild turkeys and pheasants, which all chose freedom in the land of foxes and wildcats. To accommodate our guests we built a barn, then fixed another old one.

Thus, without realizing it, we established a farm; yet we never became real farmers. I am an artist and earn my income from books and drawings, not from the products of our little enterprise. It was for us a way of collecting new experiences, curiosity about what we had never done before. Besides, it seemed that the only way to exorcise the past life was to start a new one.

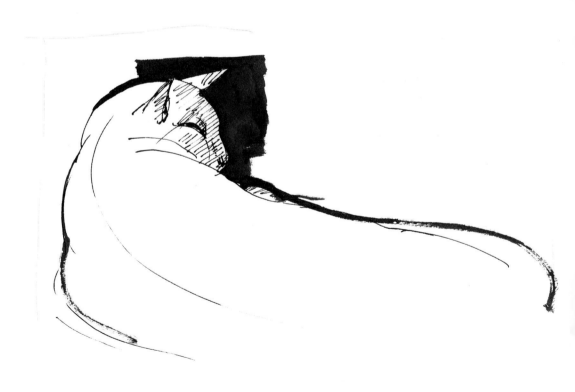

During the first three years on our peninsula I jotted and sketched what I heard with my eyes and what I saw with my ears. Any exaggerations are those of my interlocutors and the bouncing echo of local gossip. These gleanings do not give a true picture, since one always lies by omission.

And anyway . . . .

As my wife said the other day, 'one always exaggerates by telling the truth'.

I decided to keep a diary for a whole year: this was on the 29th of September 1974, the day with which the following record begins. My narrative is made up of this diary interspersed with flashbacks.

Got up at 7.30 after breakfast in bed. Went down to the cellar to turn and clean the goat cheeses. Joined Yvonne who was busy cleaning the barn, and after a spell on the dungpile went back to the studio to draw. Yvonne had already cleaned the pigsty when I returned to the barn. Put some order in the woodpile and started building more rabbit cages.

Let the goats in around the compound to eat the thistles. Brought in the sheep to pick the ones to be sold. A guy came and bought two head for thirty-eight dollars each.

10 a.m. There is a whiff and a sniff of autumn in the air. Most fall flowers here are yellow, as if to store up some of the summer's glow. That feeling of latent insecurity, brittleness, shaky as a leaf in a world of pine needles . . . . Then helped Yvonne caulk the dory. During the last storm it had crashed against some unforeseen rocks.

After that I drove to town to pick up the mail. A funny sight: last night someone had driven off the road, obviously at full speed. The car had very neatly chopped down four telephone poles. A masterpiece of karate or modern art. The poles are lying on their backs by the roadside in an attitude of patient submissiveness. The car tracks are sharply printed in the grass and the pole stumps are exactly in the middle of the tracks. Nobody knows who did it, nor ever will. The mystery of mischief adds spice to this roadside enigma.

Back home: low tide. Drove the sheep back to the Island and mended the Island fence. A good thing I did, for along came the horses trying to get on to it too. 'Sorry boys, all booked for the night. Try the Hilton, they usually have some space left.' . . .

The tides roll in and the Island is an island again.

Yvonne is busy training Keleah, a young horse, on the beach . . . she is lunging him. A lovely sight. The horse has four matching white socks. I cannot wait for the first snow: how funny a sight the horse will be from a distance, seeming to walk on his knees in mid-air, since the lower parts of his legs will match the color of the snow in a kind of jambed mimeticism.

Went back to the barn to build a partition in one of the stalls and crashed my nose into a plank. Walked back to the house in the catchup glow of a lingering sunset which matched my bleeding nose. Read the paper: Nixon has phlebitis; it's about time, for the man who himself was for so long a clot in the White House. He occupies ten rooms in the hospital . . . either he is a very big man, or the rooms are very small . . . .

All this reminds me of our cheeses.... The goats will be running dry soon and we want to preserve as many cheeses as possible.... In an old edition of the *Journal Rustique des Dames* (1868) we discovered a recipe advising us to boil some hay in a salty brine, to line a crock with this hay and stack up the cheeses inside with layers of hay in between. So we moved them into the hay as prescribed. It makes me feel like a slumlord.

Yvonne bakes fresh bread. Some smells, or to be pedantic, effluvia, have more volume, more contour, than others. The smell of bread is definitively rotund, maternally jovial.... Then back to the worst of realities – not Nixon, but lice. Yvonne has to disinfect my scalp. I was drawing, and little particles kept parachuting onto my paper. Under the scrutiny of a magnifying glass they turned out to be a clan of varmints, to whom I had been playing host as well as hostage. There is an epidemic of lice in the immediate area, and it has nothing to do with cleanliness.... It all came from a colony of emigrants who had settled in the lining of my old cap, the one I bought years ago in Hamburg. I threw the cap into the fire.

the dory

We live on a stretch of land called Rockhead. Most of our neighbor-friends are Rockheaders, and most Rockheaders are fishermen, loners who operate their own small boats. You will not find many Rockheaders working on trawlers.

'Up here we are free people! I was a young man and started working at the fisheries, and they wouldn't give us a three-cent raise, so I quit. It was in April, the air was ever so fresh and clear and I got myself some nets and rowed off in my dory and been a fisherman ever since . . . .'

This is Keene Archer talking, a friend who lives up the shore. He used to own the land on which we live. He stayed in our house when I had to go away. He is a man of cool bearing and courage . . . . He keeps his cool behind dark glasses, and when he talks his thin lips hardly move. His words seem to find their way out through his nasal passages.

In the middle of winter, during our absence, our whole flock of geese flew away on a whim and settled on a rocky ledge about a mile and a half offshore. So Keene filled a bucket with corn and started rowing our dory towards the colony of exiles. The boat had a hole in it, which Keene didn't know about, since it was sealed with ice. He was halfway out into the bay when the ice melted after coming into contact with the salt water, and the boat sprang a leak.

'I'd row three or four times, then I'd scoop out some water and then row again . . . . See?'

It never occurred to him to turn back; he went right on till he reached the ledge. He showed the corn to the geese, and they followed him in a solemn parade as he scooped and oared his way back . . . .

I met Keene on the road this morning. The weather was bad for fishing, and he had just been through a lot of trouble: 'We was out fishing and the seas, they started churning so badly, my boy he got so seasick and he was half paralyzed and I took him back to shore but then I had to git back to my nets and I took my brother along and he fell overboard and it was the air in his hip boots that kept him floating, upside-down, and my! the trouble I had hauling him back in the boat, the sides are so high, see?'

And the trip out before that one he had gone out to sea not realizing that someone had stolen the fuel out of his tank . . . . Luckily some fellow fisherman saw him drifting and towed him back on a line.

Brave new world

Keene used to raise sheep. He taught us how to shear, kill, and dress a carcass. He was the one I called on the telephone at the time of our first lambing difficulties. We had a ewe who just had no strength left to bring her lamb out into this promised land. She was lying there on the floor heaving, death sooting her almond eyes, so we called Keene.

'Now you hurry down to the barn, wash your hands well, then feel your way in till you can feel the hooves of the front legs ; get hold of them and pull the lamb out gently . . . .'

These were the only instructions we had to go by, and they triumphantly sufficed, with Yvonne holding the flashlight. It was a nigh-on spiritual experience, this thrill of being instrumental in the giving of life. It was like the uncorking of a rare *millésime* vintage . . . . Out and about five minutes later, the lamb was wobbling on its stiff legs, wagging its tail and already tapping its mother's natural resources.

natures morte

Keene is a very religious man, and he believes that sheep were biblically destined to be slaughtered and sacrificed. According to him, sheep do not know pain. I sometimes wonder if pain is non-existent for certain people as well.

I was having a little stroll by the harbor and met this fisherman, so we started a bit of a chat about the weather and lobsters . . . .

'There's only one third of the lobster there usetah be.'

'So bad, eh.'

'Well, we gets paid more for 'em, so we just put out more traps.'

'But more traps means less lobster next year.'

'Nothin' teh worry about, thar's always unemployment money.'

So we keep on talking for a while, he finally says, 'I'd better be going now and do somethin' about it . . . .'

And he shows me his hand, stigmatized by a fish-hook that has gone right through the palm.

On the ground a pool of blood testifying to the length of our yarns . . . .

'So that's the kind of bait you are using these days? I wouldn't make a habit of it . . . .'

Most fishermen do not know how to swim or float. It is part of their pride to disregard safety measures. If anything happens, it happens . . . .

A man falls overboard during a fishing trip.

Quote: 'We threw him a line and brought him back on board, he drowned on the following trip anyway . . . .'

Here today . . . gone tomorrow.

A man slips off the gangplank and drowns between hull and wharf. Do you suppose anyone has a piece of rope around here?

Two summers ago Lindy, a thirteen-year-old friend of ours, came running out of breath to the house: a little girl was drowning off the main beach. Lindy knew we could swim, and besides, Yvonne used to be a lifeguard. So we ran down: it was too late. The shore was crowded with onlookers, nonchalantly waiting for something to 'show up'. There was one man in the water looking for the body.

'Who is it?'

'Some kid.'

A few months back Yvonne had gone down in the morning to the barn, which is built right on the shore. She came back shouting, 'There is a body by the barn'. Yes, there was a body by the barn, washed in by the tide, face down in the sand. Gray socks, gray pants, gray shirt, gray hair in the gray sand under a gray sky.

Death that day was gray, anonymously so, no-man's-land gray . . . .

We called the Mounties, who called the doctor, who pronounced the dead officially dead. Then the body was removed. Its face left an exact imprint in the sand – too bad I had no plaster of Paris to fill the mold. There was some blood that had found its way through the nostrils and formed a pool in the imprint of the face giving a touch of color after all.

The police came back several weeks later with a hand-written piece of paper, which Yvonne had to sign to the effect that she had found the body of so-an'-so on the date of such and such.

. . . Gone today, gone tomorrow.

A young neighbor of ours from over the hill went off with his wife on a little driving spell, and a drinking spell as well. They had their two children with them, one of them a baby. After a spin in the woods they went down to the beach, where the car bellied itself into the sand. So the young couple left the car and walked home. The tide rolled in, and that in itself would wash this story off the shore and off the records if somewhere during their binge they had not lost the baby. Couldn't remember if he was left in the car or lost somewhere in the sticks. The matter was dragged into court. I understand the judge told them not to do it again.

The local paper published in Newbridge, the county seat, remains perfectly oblivious to what is happening in the area. I call it the *Ostrich Weekly*. As an example of front-page news we have a story headlined: 'Many Memories'.

This big hunk of a front page news item (call it a scoop) consists of an interview with Maud Crank, who has now been working for twenty years in the local general store (something like a Woolworths). Quote:

'In these twenty years you worked here, did anything happen worth telling about?'

'Yes! What comes to my mind in my years of service in this store is the time when the roof leaked, some counters had to be cleared, and I mopped the floor.'

A life of unmolested mediocrity in a world where everything is molested but mediocrity.

Other news items include the listing of visitors, tea parties, prayer parties, church news, and sports results.

Bowling is a favorite pastime here, especially among ladies. I noted down the names of some of the local teams: Moonbeams, Stardust, Sunshiners, Rainbows – teams with spatial overtones. Then the Butterballs, Untouchables, Rat Patrol, Snorkels, and of all things the Imports. Where do these come from? . . . Dunno!

Occasionally, though, some newsworthy items do find their way into the paper . . . . Mrs MacLard, a sizeable older woman, went into the woods to collect mushrooms. She bent down to pick some and wedged herself between the trunks of two sturdy trees. Unable to dislodge herself, she remained there two days till somebody found her. The story does not mention whether they had to chop down one of the trees, or what happened to the mushrooms. As for the lady, I assume that she must have been fat, and that after having been on a forced diet for a while, she would have lost enough weight to slip away, unless the tree trunks formed a V . . . .

I found this story rather unusual, since people here live in mortal fear of wild mushrooms and I myself have never met a single local person who would pick fungi. This could possibly explain the wealth of mushrooms to be found unharmed in the woods. Under the spruce trees by the shore I have actually seen fields of chanterelles, and once I scooped up four pounds of them in a mere twenty minutes.

. . . Had a quiche for lunch with a scattering of shrimp in it, then drove to the garbage dump, one of my favorite places. It has a fine incinerator which always reminds me of the Strutthoff concentration camp where the Nazis turned my compatriots into garbage. Here it is the other way around: you put in the garbage and after combustion you end up with a nice pile of rusted metal and molten glass, ideal for my sculptures.

'Drop the past into bygones, and forge the future young man!'

That's what we are doing, especially since a friend of mine offered me a big anvil that was in his garage. This friend is a very strong man: he drove in one day in one of his trucks, unloaded the anvil and dropped it at my feet, and I can't even budge the thing. Yvonne and I are not only forging the future but a few other things as well, like latches for the stalls and such things. On Wednesdays we drive to Newbridge and take an evening course in welding and metalwork. The first thing I made was a large fork for the fireplace. One of my fellow pupils was watching me with strained and sieved curiosity, then finally muttered: 'Some heavy eat'n'. The second item was a branding iron with my trademark $\overline{U}$ – to mark my wife, my models and my cattle. . . . Needless to say I never used it, and besides I did such a bad welding job that the T fell off the first time I dropped the thing on the floor.

The dump is also a treasure trove for pieces of metal, screws, bolts, wheels and of course discarded ovens, fridges and furniture. No matter how poor the area, the dump is still a showcase for the consumer society. We found there two lovely metal bedsteads. At one point, luckily just as we were fixing our house, there was a craze to get rid of old-fashioned panelled doors and replace them with new hollow plywood nonentities. All we had to do was collect some doors and bring them home. The garbage collector is a friend of ours, and we can practically place our orders for this or that. The man who runs the incinerator was born on our little island. There used to be a house there, and a waterhole which once played host to my publisher, Daniel Keel.

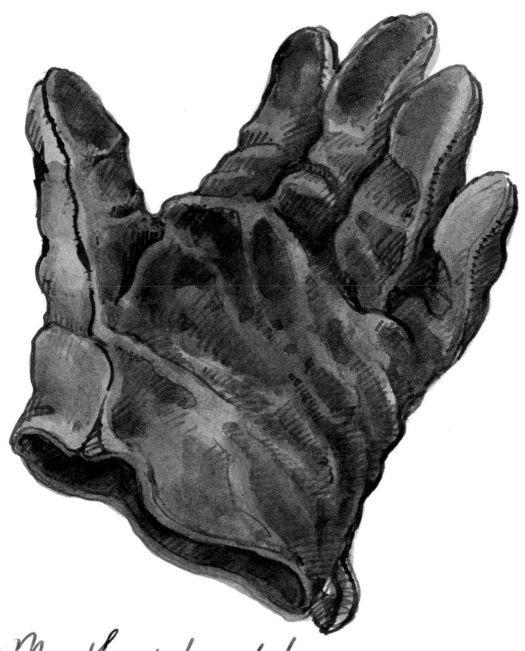

My third hand!
a palm reader's challenge.—

It was in the icy core of winter. Monsieur Keel was on hand to take pictures of us carrying bales of hay to the sheep. To get the picture into focus he took a few steps backward, not knowing that the waterhole was yawning there under the layer of snow. He disappeared as he snapped the picture. We urged him to run home as fast as possible before he turned into a crystal chandelier with pneumonia.

The man manning the incinerator says: 'Yes, there even used to be a little bridge planking us to the mainland . . . .' He tells me about the past, the storms, the hard times, no food, no fuel, and the day when 'my littler sister she fell off the bridge and all you could see was her little white hands waving goodbye out of the churning waters . . . .'

Memories around here are laundered in a lot of 'churning waters'.

Stitch is our nearest neighbor. He lives on Rockhead road, just where our driveway starts, in a new bungalow to which he retired with his wife, Sadie.

Stitch is a gossip and storyteller of twisted originality. He is the only landlubber on Rockhead, and that somewhat singles him out. In his working life he was a farmer, gardener and woodsman. Stitch will have nothing to do with fishing. He stepped into a boat once, didn't like it, and that was the end of it. But if Stitch was born finless he certainly has the compensation of a green thumb. The greenest thumb I have ever seen . . . .

Stitch came down to our place for a little visit. Whenever he comes, he first goes to the fridge and checks its contents . . . .

'Had mashed potatoes for lunch?'

Yvonne: 'Yes Stitch, we had mashed potatoes for lunch.'

I am upstairs in my studio sitting at my desk. The trap door is open and I am eavesdropping and jotting down the exchange.

Stitch sits down at the table.

Yvonne: 'Stitch, would you like some cookies?' She had just baked a batch of chocolate chip cookies.

Stitch: 'Yooh wemen folks are all the same, yooh just offer me cookies for me to tell yooh how good they are.'

Yvonne says nothing, I hear her putting away some dishes . . . .

Stitch: 'Well Yevohn, how about those cookies?'

Yvonne: 'I am not giving you any because that's not the reason why I offered them to you.'

A silence; Stitch finally splits it with a well-sharpened remark; annoyed or frustrated by a lack of cookies, he has to say something derogatory: 'Your pigs, they'll gain no weight!'

Yvonne: 'How can that be?'

Stitch: 'They are kept too clean. Clean pigs gain no weight, 'tis the Lord's truth.' For Stitch anything that can be questionable is automatically the Lord's truth, obviously not his . . . .

Yvonne says nothing, she knows better. Our animals are well kept, well fed, and Yvonne, who loves animals, tends them well. They thrive under her warm-hearted leadership. The only ones which have left us were the pheasants and wild turkeys which, as I already mentioned, escaped to the woods.

Our pigs are clean because pigs are clean by instinct. They always agree to shit in the same corner, which makes it extremely easy to clean their pen. They pass for dirty because outside they roll in the mud. This is necessary since their bodies are not protected by hair, and their bare skin tends to dry and crack in the summer, not to mention sunburns and bug bites. Mud is the only natural protection they have.

Pigs are intelligent animals with endearing personalities. Easy to train, in by-gone times they used to be one of the main attractions in travelling circuses . . . .

I finally come down from the studio.

'Hello Stitch, what's new, what's going on . . . ?'

'Well I just come down to tell you one of your cows is on heat.' Right now they are grazing in a pasture across the road, opposite Stitch's house.

'And how can you tell?'

'Because she behaves like a lesbian . . . .'

Which is exactly what they do, trying to mount the other cows from behind. 'A good thing our wives don't do the same, right Stitch, can you imagine Sadie behaving like that, once a month . . . ?'

The conversation goes on. Stitch tells us of the days when he used to work on a dairy farm in Annapolis Valley and how they had no use for the newborn calves and just threw them alive into the pen as feed for the pigs, and how on Rockhead the fishermen used to feed their pigs mackerel . . . .

Year after year, one of our main activities is to clear woods to extend the pasture land. There are lots of trees and brush to cut down. Some of the wood is cut into fencing posts or firewood. The rest, huge piles of branches, has to be dragged away to be burned on the beach. To help us we have gangs of local kids who come down after school to earn some money. We have a bit of fun as well, making huge bonfires. Once we roasted a whole lamb on a·spit, another time I brought out my supply of bandages and sent all the kids home disguised as casualties with fake blood – the parents, at first shocked, had their laughs over it . . . .

Angus and Toby Logan are two brothers from a large fisherman's family on Rockhead. They come over regularly to help. Angus is twelve, Toby two years older.

We are working away cutting brush and making piles when Angus stops and says, 'Tom, would ye have a band-aid?'

'Why, what's the matter, did you hurt yourself?'

'Broke me finger . . . broke me finger yesterday.'

'Yesterday, and you didn't go and see the doctor?'

'Nope.'

'Now listen to me, a band-aid is of no use for a broken finger, go home and tell your mother to take you to the doctor.'

They leave, reluctantly it seems. Angus' finger looks a mess all right, infected as well as broken . . . .

Two weeks or so go by. The two boys show up again for some work . . . .

Yvonne asks, 'How is your finger?'

'Oh, it's healing all right.'

'What did you do to it?' says Yvonne, looking at the twisted stumpy mess.

'Toby fixed it, pulled out the nail with a pair of pliers!'

Yvonne: 'That must have hurt terribly?'

Angus: 'Yap, just took a deep breath.'

Now what does the pulling out of a fingernail have to do with a broken finger? I fetched the camera and took a portrait of Angus displaying his finger with a big proud smile. Fancy having the snapshot printed as a postcard: 'Souvenir from Nova Scotia, Atlantic playground'. 'Atlantic playground' is the official trade mark for the province and it is stamped on every car licence plate . . . . It is exactly the way we feel about our life here, playful, grounded, and oceanic . . . .

A quote overheard at the doctor's office:

'A bit of pain wouldn't hurt you.'

A lot of people here are refractory about medical aid for religious reasons. Blood transfusions especially are considered one of Satan's fluid tricks. Doctors are thought to offer unfair competition to faith healers.

A teacher told me of a little girl who had been out of school for three weeks. It was then found that she had gone unattended with a broken leg.

Excerpt from a song [Roy Acuff]:

I fixed it up with Jesus,
A long, long time ago . . . .

twin flower

It is always a very special day when Gordon Twight comes to visit to shoe the horses. He is a blacksmith of the old school. He looks ancient and squints with his one remaining eye, through which you can see the glow of his inner forge. 'It takes thirty years to master a trade, to know horses, to know iron: you must be better than iron, to beat in.' His know-how reaches an instinctive level, and the most nervous horse calms right down when it enters his aura. Gordon brings his wife along, and they stay for lunch. She is an upright woman, her voice as clear as her wintry eyes.... 'My mother, when we killed the pig she locked herself up in the house and played the harmonium.'

Pig killing is always a great topic of conversation. Actually, they say around here that it is bad luck to use the word 'pig': the proper substitute is 'Mister Dennis'. You can imagine the dismay of outsiders eavesdropping on natives discussing the killing of Mister Dennis....

This brings me to transcribe a little monologue on the subject which I jotted down. It comes from Stitch as we sat down for what he calls a 'little blow', meaning a break in our work . . . .

'Now my father he was "jist terrahfied" when the time come to kill Mister Dennis, and he would go and hide behind the barn till it was over. We had one of them guns that you loaded by the muzzle with black powder, and it shot a round "bullitt" which you packed on top of the powder. Now I sneaked behind the critter and put the gun to his head and I pulled the trigger and there! There was a puff and a huff of smoke and the bullitt hit Mister Dennis behind the ear and bounced off leaving a blue mark. My! It got some cautious after that, I had to wait ten minutes to kill it again! And my old dad he stayed behind the barn all the time . . . .

'I had my first pig [Mr Dennis already gone into oblivion] the year I got married, that's when granpah died after chopping wood on the ice wearing his cowhide mocassins.

[These are not mocassins but a kind of spats. When a cow was killed they used to pull the hide off the lower legs. This with the hairy part turned to the inside would make a kind of muff into which you slipped your feet.]

'Well then, his feet took to swelling, then they cracked and started to ooze away. Doctor Bogwood he came and he said to granmah Orkis, "keep them oozing, keep them oozing. As long as they will flow he'll count among the living . . . ."

'They oozed for some time yet. Then by and by they stopped giving out water and he died. My daughter she sent me a book of poems called *Old Country Roads.*' Stitch sits back in the grass, shuts his eyes, and starts down memory Lane:

> I want to live in a house
> by the side of the road,
> and be a friend to man . . . .

'Well Stitch,' I can't help interrupting him, 'you live in a house by the side of the road but you can't be friend to man because no one likes you, that's what you always complain about, no friends . . . .'

Stitch likes to read and loves music. When he plays the accordion he sits on the very edge of a chair and bends forward, so low that one has the impression that the accordion is crawling on the ground like a spastic caterpillar. In a copy-book he has neatly transcribed his repertoire of songs. When he sets out to sing he will stand up straight as a bean pole, with one arm behind his back and the other outstretched holding the book. He looks like an example for a posture class.

Stitch and his family are Jehovah's Witnesses. One of his sons is a preacher of that faith. The son and his family were visiting there one day and *Planet of the Apes* was on television. We made the remark that it was not so far-fetched, since our ancestors too had been monkeys of one kind or another. That statement crashed like a cobblestone into a fishbowl. 'No no, the world was created in . . . .' (I forget the date.) The mother, appalled, took her little boy in her arms. 'We ain't no monkeys are we, no dearie? We are no monkeys. Does your mommy look like a monkey? No she don't . . . .'

We left, bending our backs under the downpour of irrefutable arguments.

Stitch doesn't listen to what you have to say, or, if he does, he will repeat it as if it came out of his own thinking.

. . . On with the monologue: 'In them days we cut wood for a living and one day I was in town delivering some firewood to this here lady, wealthy folks ye know, and she invites me in for a bite, me and my brother, because I was working with my brother then. Now my mother she was a hard workin' woman; baked bread every day, knitted all our socks and sweaters, mended our clothes at night, but she told us too about manners . . . some manners. So me and my brother we sat tight and we knew better than to put our elbows on the table or our hands, see? But anyway each time I put my hands on the table it would take an incline, like a ship, so I ask'd my brother "Did you see that?" – "Yes," he explained, "this here table is mounted on a swivel, it keeps you from havin' bad manners."'

There is a pause. Stitch sits up and looks at me as if he suddenly notices my presence. 'Now, tell me, isn't that something?' (pronounced 'somthn').

I told Stitch that in France it was bad manners not to have your hands on the table, otherwise you might be suspected of feeling up your lady neighbor or even yourself for that matter . . . . We had our laughs and went back to work, cutting posts for a fence. Stitch is a real woodman. I drool with envy watching the blade of his axe sink into the wood as if it were mere cheese. It takes me four blows to one of his to cut a piece of wood. Then we stretched a few strands of barbed wire around the new pasture. Since I grew up in war-torn Europe it always seems strange to see barbed wire used for peaceful purposes, and I imagine a few trenches and some pill-boxes as well, to protect our tract of land.

Finished the fencing and drove the cows into their new compound. They are in splendid shape, so is Yvonne, so am I.

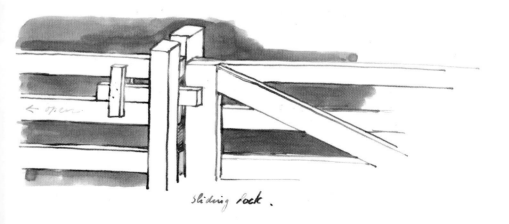

sliding lock.

Evening stroll on the beach . . . the sun is low, stretching our shadows like rubber bands. Our legs on the sand look like pantyhose hanging on the washline to dry.

The life of a shadow: its complete dependence on its master, not allowed to make a single move on its own. A shadow is a kind of parasite that lives off you. The stronger the light the more obstinately it clings to you.

The horses' manes and tails seem to have caught fire in the sunset.

Stretched out on my side in the beachgrass and had a stare at the sea. The line of the horizon has become a vertical one, and everything has shifted into relativity.

41

Discreet arrival of the autumn, always premature here. The sky is a pale, javel-bleached, washed-out blue, already refined by the cold air currents. High above, the season is taking the veil, piously. Close to the earth, hugging its contours, a mild breeze stirs memories.

Change of seasons, anticlimates and anticlimax. Summer as a season melts away in its own complacent heat, giving way for the fall. This arrangement seems to be an amiable one, the result of peaceful deterioration.

For a while the two seasons even blend, till summer finally flows out into retirement, leaving the new management to handle the liquidation.

Autumn files the petition for summer's bankruptcy.

Winter comes with an onset. It does not knock on the door, but rather knocks it down. There is something martial about winter. Of all the seasons the one against which most defences are needed. Winter does not easily give up the fight. It will fight back with counterattacks and leave pockets of resistance behind.

The spring, insidious, all inside work, fifth column; sap is flowing behind the lines to feed the buds, which will suddenly explode into leaves and flowers. And then what a display! Nothing is as arrogant as a shy person who has overcome shyness.

The senses, which have been hiding, surface: bubbling, throbbing, tumescent. The come of spring finally sizzles in the summer's frying pants.

Summer takes it for granted . . . .

Spring is nice for birth and weddings, and one should die in the fall, with winter as second choice.

Smashy is fourteen. He looks like an urchin and is up to no good. He came down to borrow twenty dollars . . . .

'Twenty dollars! What do you want this money for?'

'To buy a car.'

'For twenty dollars? You must be kidding.'

'Nope . . . .'

Well it was not the first time he borrowed money from us and he always paid it back in work, so off he went with two ten-dollar bills wriggling in his pocket.

As for the car, he did buy it, and what a car . . . ! With no doors, no roof, and an engine whose noise made up for all the missing features. A rolling ghost of a wreck. The most original detail was the radiator, which was held in place with a nylon rope . . . . Of course whenever the engine took to overheating the nylon melted and the rope had to be replaced. I do not remember the rope ever being replaced with a heatproof piece of wire.

Smashy drove his car like a dragon. The beach to our house was used at the time for some very wild driving. Since then we have blocked its access with boulders.

On a car sticker in Ireland I read 'Drive like hell, and you'll get there'.

As it is, to watch the local boys drive is an infernal sight.

Fancy, crippled in a car accident, drags himself around hunched over a pair of crutches. He is a lovely good-humored loafer, with a tender and sensitive face framed by a beard. If he could afford a nightshirt he would easily pass for a prophet.

Put him in a car and our Jekyll turns into a thousand roaring Hydes, with of course as much rum as gasoline being volatilized in the experience.

You could at times see him drive in as tightly spun circles as his speed would allow, actually on two smoking wheels, till the car would break down. Then you would see Fancy shoulder his way out of the fuming car, slam the hood open and hit the exposed, defenceless engine in the crotch with a crutch and, believe it or not, the car would always start after such a beating. We found out later, my wife and I, that the trick works on children as well.

I was reminded of this vision because a few nights ago we pulled Fancy's car out of a ditch. The car was full of girls slutting drunk. It seemed to confirm the reputation hump-backs have for humping . . . .

Smashy's parents had just repainted their house in blue and pink. Smashy used the leftover paint to glamorize his jalopy, so that it stood in front of the house in matching colors.

I suspect that there is some kind of conspiracy in Canada to dump all unsold stocks of paints in Nova Scotia. You will find discontinued shades of nausea lilac, loo brown, tonsil pink, Miami turquoise and cesspool green harmoniously sharing the façade of a house.

There is one house in town that is uniformly painted in one shade of olive. Over the entrance hangs a sign:
'You don't like the color of my house,
I don't like the color of yours either.'

Yvonne reports.

She had a little chat with a woman up the hill. They just had a new toilet installed to replace the old outhouse.

Yvonne: 'Bet you enjoy the comfort.'

Woman: 'Som'th'n new anyway.'

An old woman died. She lived alone, poor. Nobody claimed the body and the town was going to give her what is called a 'pauper's wedding' when it was found out that she had some savings. All of a sudden eleven relatives who were living under cover popped out of nowhere into her bloodline! They had been hiding in the foliage of her genealogical tree.

Called Mrs Solong to order some hay . . . .
'Can I speak to Mr Solong?'
'He ain't here.'
'When can I talk to him?'
'Don' know, he's dead' (*sob*).
'Dead?'
'Well yes, he burned in his bed last night, but if you are calling for some hay you'll get it all the same.'

I had applied for a rather high amount of life insurance. The company sent down an investigator who went around town to make inquiries about me. 'Who is this Tomi Ungerer?'

Someone answered, 'A writer'. This complicated and unusual word was misunderstood for 'waiter'. That ended the inquiry, since the inspector found it unlikely that a waiter could afford a policy with such high installments.

When we emigrated to Canada I had to state my profession, but neither 'author' nor 'designer' nor 'graphic artist' was to be found in the volume listing all the professions. So I was entered as 'entrepreneur': 'undertaker' would have been more to my taste.

. . . Some days are brittle and little, days for small dabble jobs; snacks replace meals, symphonies are unbearable, and even short stories are too long to read. You putter, mutter, have your hair cut, clean out old paint brushes, sort out rusty nails from the screws, mend broken dishes, kick the dog.

Days like this are between tic and tac. Minutes all have strictly the same time span and the clock keeps an exact account of every supercilious second.

Unravelling strings and sorting out the rubbish from the dump. Our kitchen light was made on a day like that: a Frankenstein lamp togethered from elements of eight different lamps, it can light up on kerosene as well as electricity. The sofa in the living room was nailed together out of leftover pieces of floorplanks: it was conceived in what we call our 'Bunker Style' or '*style Maginot*'. The sides and the back are designed to protect you from draughts and bullets. All it needs now is a little drawbridge and a few '*meurtrières*'. Speaking of bullets . . . two Japanese reporters came here for an interview. We offered them hospitality, which began with a nice roast beef dinner. They spoke hardly any English, and we carried on our conversation in a gesticulatory way. As the roast was put on the table I said, pointing to it: 'American G.I.' They thought this was very funny and giggled away like bashful maidens.

After dinner we settled them on the sofa in front of a nice fire in the fireplace. I do have bits of ammunition around the place, and a cartridge must have rolled off the mantlepiece onto the hearth.

'Bang.' It exploded in the middle of our conversation . . . and again, giggling, one of the Japs said, pointing at the fire, 'American G.I., hee hee, American G.I....'

We hadn't checked the sheep on the Island for a while. So we went to bring them back, since we had some orders for a few carcasses. Before winter people get anxious to stock up their freezers and you get a fair price for your meat.

We found one sheep dead, 'cast'. This happens when a sheep lies down in a hollow, when they are mattressed with heavy fleece. They lie on their backs, too top-heavy to roll over and stand up. With their four feet stretched up towards the clouds they starve, like turtles in a similar predicament. A dramatic sight, heightened by their hollow eye cavities, gouged out by the gourmet crows.

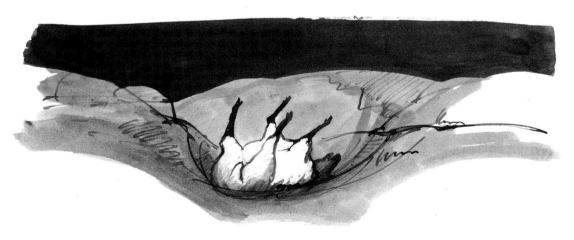

Cast !

For the killing of sheep we sometimes get help from Blade. He is an ace in skinning sheep, and I am not.

When you come in contact with a sheep, the lanolin of its fleece clings to your hands.... It is excellent for your skin; it is like a hand lotion. But lanolin has a terribly strong smell and taste, and you can spoil the taste of a sheep carcass should you touch the meat with these hands, especially on a rainy day. Blade does the job with a surgeon's touch. Yvonne and I are then merely his assistants.

It is early in the morning. The sheep are rounded up, and I call Blade at home....

'Hello? Blade?'

A woman's voice answers: 'He ain't here.'

'Can you leave him a message?'

'Not any more (*sob*), he's just died.'

What could I say to that . . . so I call Keene to ask him to give us a hand: 'Yes,' he says he'll be over this afternoon.

'Good, see you then.'

We feel really sick over the whole business, the killing of animals when a mutual acquaintance has just passed over the river Jordan, and a fellow sheep-killer at that. We feel the angel of death upon us. The sweetish, sweatish fetidness of the steaming innards rolling passively into the vat, and poor Blade who should be here with us and who will never be with us again. I throw the sheeps' heads into the sea. They float away, pinking the water, their eyes staring forgivingly....

I walk Keene up the driveway and we meet Stitch. We tell him all about poor Blade.... Yap! Here today, gone tomorrow.

Later that night the telephone rings....

Yvonne picks it up. Stitch on the line with a deep and hollowed-out voice. 'Yevohn? Well Yevohn, sm'th'n' strange is goin' on around here.'

'What is it, Stitch?'

'There seems to be total confusion.'... Silence... 'Several people in town say that they happened to see Blade today....' There is only one thing to do, and that is to dial Blade's number. His own voice answers the phone.

'Hey Blade, it's great to hear your voice, we thought you died this morning....' Been kidding him about it ever since. We never did find out who it was who had answered the phone that morning.

'Gone today, here tomorrow'.

Jay Hoke is in his forties and helps here occasionally in the building of our house extension. He acts funny in a scatter-minded way. He makes a lot of mistakes....I had a talk with him and he told me that he was terminally ill. The doctors had given him two years to live and at the moment he had already outlived himself by six months. Quote: 'Been dead six month' already.'

All this butchering is eroding the hinterland of my mind. Had a dream in which we butchered a baby (not ours) and ate it. I was thrown in jail along with my beloved wife. The dream became a rather pleasant one, since there was only one thing a healthy couple could do in solitary confinement. I seem to remember that Yvonne had more than time on her hands and that even her sister joined us in our dungeon!!

Here you are always made aware that there is a sky overhead, even inside the house, because one depends so much on the weather. To 'have sky' is a comfort of sorts. I wouldn't like to be a box without a lid or a book without a binding.

Unexpected realities overlap crossing their fibers, webbing you in.

Days progress through stage sets, the effects emphasized by the sudden changes of weather.

Today: low tide, the sheep are driven back to the Island. They run like children out of school and disappear behind a rocky ledge. The billygoat has joined the flock accidentally. Yvonne is trying to drag him back. She holds him by the horns as if he were a bicycle, by the handle bars . . . .

Go to the workshop with the foolish idea of making a violin out of a cigar box for Stitch who likes music. Hair from Rajah's tail will provide me what I need for the bow . . . .

Out again. This is a day for mirages. The sky is mirrored in the sea, and the sea is mirrored in the sky. Between them an island appears, hovering afloat between two horizon lines. Then boats defying all sense of proportion float by in mid-air and turn into castellated cliffs.

They belong to a *Club Mauditerranée* for lost souls, or maybe our own souls are there, revelling, while we sit it out on the lachrymose shores of life.

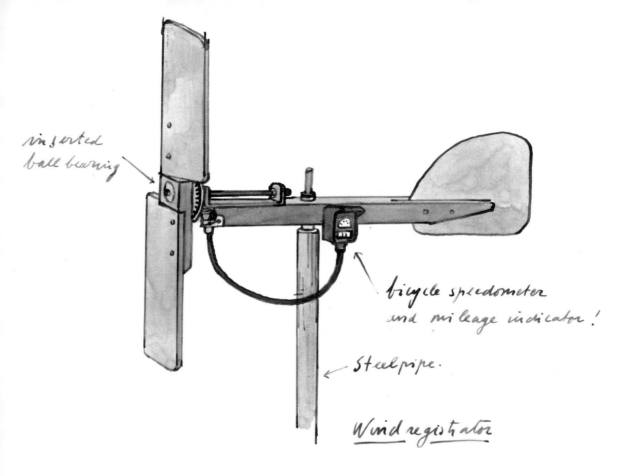

inserted
ball bearing

bicycle speedometer
and mileage indicator!

Steelpipe.

Wind registrator

The prevailing meteorology is determined by the gulf stream, mixing its tepid waters with colder ones from the north. This is a place of fast and unexpected weather changes and thick fogs, which, in the summer especially, blanket the shores for weeks.

You may find yourself in the wind, blowing from the east, yet looking up, you will see flocks of clouds driving from the west. The wind may turn about-face in no time at all and stab you in the back before you know it. I have never seen a weather vane around here . . . it wouldn't last. It would quickly lose its bearings or its marbles.

The weather here is a 'she'.

'She's goin to be sunny and dry.'

The women's liberationists may argue the point, but that's the way it is. And why not: unstable, fussy, squalling and yapping, then going into heat, turning frigid, then balmy and loving . . . .

I go down to the post office. I ask:
'What do you think of the weather?'
The lady says: 'She's bound to be dry and westerly.'
Drive home and meet Stitch, and I ask him:
'What do you think of the weather?'
'She's bound to be dry and westerly.'
'Hey Stitch, did you by any chance go to the post office this morning?'
'Why? Yes I did.'
'Just asking.' News travels fast, and Stitch passes for a bit of a barometer around here.

A truck is rolling in, loaded with timber. Croyd comes along. He unloads the wood and his sorrows. He had pleurisy three years ago, and never had time to recuperate – 'jist gotta work.' Wife is ill, she faces new operations; on top of that they had a surprise baby, ten years after the last one.

'. . . I jist can't think straight any more, life is blurry, and I have to go on, grin and bear it . . . . yap, grin and bear it . . . .' His misery has clouded my day. Wind-driven drizzle . . . from the east . . . so much for the dry westerly 'she'.

In the cellar. Checked my crocks of cheese. One of them has turned into a ghetto full of horrid grey grubs. A strange new breed which I have never set eyes on before: scaly with spikes. I am not waiting for them to turn into butterflies. They have to be forcibly evicted on the spot. They offer no resistance, and protests are ignored with a pinched sneer, as I relish the pickled arrogance of power.

The other cheeses are excellent.

The rest of the day focusses on Yvonne and me, in the kitchen confecting patés. Some Germans are coming for a visit, and we have decided to welcome them with an 'Adolf-Hitler-Pastete' or Paté 'Meinkampf'. When you slice it on a plate it displays the outline of a swastika in white fat inserted in a circle of red ham.

The Germans arrived. We fed them our commemorative delicacy and put them to bed. (I must specify here that one of them was Robert Pütz, who later became a very good friend, collaborator and godfather to our daughter.) It is early October, but in the middle of the night Yvonne and I wake up: a sound of muffled droning, and of pins and needles being thrown against the window. It's not the Germans, it's the She-weather. Mother Blizzard. Just in time to welcome our guests to this beautiful shore. In the morning we wake up to an avalanche of emergencies. A blizzard in October!! Soon the power goes. Wires, poles and trees start to snap. It is always the best trees, the ones you spared when clearing the woods, which suffer the most. Driven by the wind, the snow piles up on one side of the tree till branches or trunks break under the weight. There is no time to cry over it; anyway, the tears would freeze. On the upper pasture we find the cows in two feet or more of snow.... I open the gate, planning to drive them to the protective reclusion of the barn. Forget it! The flatulent idiots, in a state of bovine stupor, run off in the opposite direction, towards Rockhead. The Germans are a great help in rounding them up . . . . Running in high snow was the closest I ever came to heart failure. We got them in, us in, and huddled around the fireplace. On the radio the province was proclaimed to be in a state of emergency, which is a state of mind as well; possibly even a good one if I think of the good creative work we produced.

Mother Blizzard finally left us as suddenly as she had showed up.

Cotton wool silence. The crows are the first to emerge from hiding to give the landscape a touch of color.

The sheep! We forgot all about the sheep. They have vanished altogether. We look around, calling them, and we finally hear a muffled, bleating answer . . . from under the snow. They had found a shelter behind a rock ledge and the snow had drifted over them and completely covered them up. We dig a hole and out they pour from their igloo.

The fall: a season of wholesale slaughter. It is an economic necessity, since we cannot feed an overstocked farm over the winter. First the rabbits. We only keep Pudding, the mother of all mothers, and the biggest buck. This mass killing is celebrated with a dish of little rabbit kidneys rolling around in a pan, puddled with wine sauce.

Then the ducks. Our ducks are mallards and black-ducks, the local wild breed. They cross and give us malblacks. All of them good to eat, they live in freedom in the pond and on the shore. An occasional feeding of grain is enough to persuade them to stay. In the fall we lure them with corn into the barn, for selective killing. The ones we eat are the young ones, six months old, *âge tendre*. Wild in taste and tame between your teeth . . . . They will hibernate in our freezer.

Then the chickens . . . and then the geese. That is a tragedy. We have a special affection for these birds. They mate for life, and one has to be careful not to break up a marriage . . . . After the killings we visit our neighbors and drop off some of our victims. There is a codeless system of bartering which weaves the fabric of our neighborly relations.

We drive up to Rockhead to drop a goose off at Sunny Logan's (Angus' and Toby's father) and to ask him to give Stitch and me a hand in killing a cow.

Sten, one of the younger boys, is there. Not in school: he was sent back home the first day with a note from the teacher saying that he should be sent to an institution because he is deaf and dumb.

Quote: 'We thought he was kind of quiet now, wasn't he?'

Sunny Logan is a fisherman, smallish, sturdy, rather Germanic looking; he laughs well and easily. This is how I met him. We had not been long in Nova Scotia when one night the phone rang. It was already dark.

'You Younger?' (The name Ungerer is too quaint a throat-clearing word for the locals and 'Younger' is the logical shortcut and a fitting one besides because I feel younger every day since I came here.)

'You Younger?'

'Yes, why?'

'You meet me down the beach?'

'Well, yes . . . .' It was low tide. So I drove down, apprehensive about what was going on: someone picking a fight, a rendezvous with destiny?

A pick-up truck with dimmed lights was already lurking in the dark, when I arrived, and Sunny, whom I didn't know, sat in it, waiting.

'Got a crate of lobster for ye.'

'That's terrific! How much do you want for it?'

'I want nothing! You're nice to us, we are nice to you.'

With Stitch and Sunny we kill the cow.

We take turns sawing down the spine . . . . Talk about a hard job. Some people use a power saw, but it's dangerous and messy. A cow is not a tree. We get the job done; Sunny drives home, and I linger awhile with old Stitch, who mutters and shakes his head . . . . 'Logans . . . thems Logans . . . thems Logans . . . Logans . . . . (*deep sigh*) thems Logans . . . .'

I can feel that he is percolating something.

'Well Stitch, for heaven's sake, you want to say something, why don't you speak up and say it?'

'Thems Logans, them is awful sexy people.'

'How is that? How can you tell?'

'They do it all the time . . . . Now, you take my wife, she used to run a canteen up the road, you know, around here. Now any time a Logan would walk in, he'd get so excited after a little while, he would get so excited he'd get up and leave, got so excited he couldn't stand it, to stay there and have a cup of tea . . . .'

'How could one know it was excitement?'

'Oh, you could see them bulge in their pants, yes bulge in their pants . . . 'tis the Lord's truth . . . .'

Sex Maniac!

We funerated the departure of our cow with a *pot-au-feu* followed the next day by a dish of *Orgelpfiffe* (organ pipes). When I was little I could choose the dish I wanted for my birthday, and this was the one. You take the leftovers from the *pot-au-feu*, meat and vegetables, and chop them very fine with fresh parsley. Then you make a batch of *crêpes*. Put the chopped stuffing on the *crêpe* and roll it into a cylinder. Slice the cylinder into three equal parts and set them upright into a deep timbale dish. Grate some cheese on top of the whole thing (you can pour some cream on top of it as well), and then into the oven . . . .

To cook with one's own products, home-raised and home-grown, is a kind of *poésie vérité et méritée*. Where meals have the *consistance* of the *circonstance* . . . .

The same *poésie* goes into the confection of patés, or the smoking of hams or fish.

I am sure that the souls of the animals whose lives were shortened around this place find redemption through our ultimate digestive process.

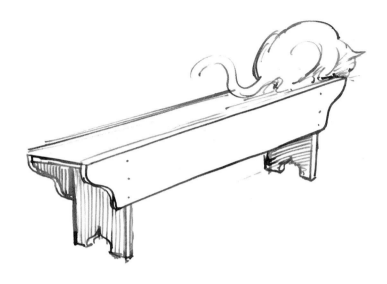

A questionnaire sent out to authors for some kind of reference book arrived. One question was 'Hobbies': I answered: 'My wife and butchering....' I have hundreds of hobbies and I wrote this answer just for effect, but still there is a spine of truth in it. In piecing out a carcass you are surgeon, anatomist, gourmand, assassin, high priest.... This accumulation of trades has its own side-effects of snobbery. I tend to sneer at people who talk and write about food when you, as butcher, are the only one who really knows, from the feeding, from the sticking, down to the dish, what food *really* can be . . . meaning that really to be able to enjoy an omelette one should know how it feels to lay an egg....

For me a roast has personality of its own, a cheese can become a pet, and some cheeses can turn into self-indulgent grumpy misfits, wretched sinners you have to rinse and rub with salt.

The pigs I have drawn as an artist are pigs I have killed and butchered myself.

There is something quite Gothic about a carcass. Is it the ogive formed by the exposed ribcage hanging upside-down? Or is it that death is always Gothic? It certainly is not *art déco*, and the Renaissance is already too flippant a style to reflect efficiently the finality of death.

Drawing and cutting up meat have a similar need for incisive precision. What is cut cannot be uncut.

The purity of one's appetite is gastronomically essential. With an appetite adulterated by stress and worries, smudged with city grime, you cannot really appreciate a meal.

I am always driven to talk compulsively about that 'high' state of earned gastro-autonomy. And I find, very presumptuously, that we eat best at home. Dishes are concocted, or better tailored to fit, in privacy. I really enjoy a meal only when I am alone with my other half, meaning my wife. A guest is always an intruder, but worse yet is to eat alone.

The bouquet of a wine really comes out when you share it.

Another element is the freedom of action, of inventiveness. You have a limited variety of supplies, so you have to make up, invent, substitute. The French are stiff-necked. Their foods are predictable. They take eating much too seriously to be able to enjoy it. Giggles cramp my throat when I hear that a *nouvelle cuisine* has been 'discovered'. (In China?) A *cuisine* is always *nouvelle* when it is good and simple and healthy and improvised.

But offer a Frenchman a poached salmon with an aioli sauce, served with a bordeaux just because you feel like it, and you'll see his face disappear into the gap of his own grimace. Serve him a goulash and there is the dire risk that he has never even heard of paprika.

Trinke ... etc ...
vom goldenen Überfluss der Welt.

Events which mark the oncoming of winter:

Snowbuntings arrive in flurries of snowballs.

Then Mrs McFlaw breaks her leg . . . this due to the ice on her steps as well as the ice in her gin.

Then with the first frost all the trouble with Diamond Lil. Diamond Lil is a duck, so called for the display of diamond-shaped feathers upon her well-rounded chest. Normal ducks fly around the place and land on the frozen surface of the pond. After a skid they get up and walk away. Not Diamond Lil. She simply has never figured out how to walk on the ice, nor has she devised a technique for taking off. So there she is on her stomach, doing the splits, helplessly waiting like a fossilized ballerina. Waiting for what? Waiting for us, of course, to grab some stones and lapidate and break the newly-formed ice around her, till she finds her-

self afloat. This works out well near the shore, when the ice is still thin and provided we don't hit our star-studded duck. But then as the ice gets thicker we need bigger and bigger stones and finally the day comes when the ice has become stone-resistant but will not yet carry the weight of a human being.

What a circus! We then have to stretch a rope across the pond, tie it to the row-boat and tug it towards the stranded fowl.

The most important event, the real inauguration of our winter, is the slaughtering of the first pig. You need freezing weather for the carcass to seize; the auspicious date usually falls at the November full moon. You get a better bleed by the full moon .... That is why if I were a general I'd always plan my offensives for a full moon ....

It is quite a job to kill a pig and dress it, more so for a man and a woman alone with only each other's help.

We started raising pigs and then were faced with the fact that there was nobody around here to do a proper job. What they do here is shoot them without even bleeding them. We looked for books, instructions, advice, and found none but a booklet published by the Morton Salt Company. There we were told that a pig should not be nervous or excited before the kill because then the blood flows out to the extremities. You can tell right away when a pig is excited because it blushes as easily as a Victorian virgin facing her first four-letter-word.

After the kill the beast should be hoisted upside-down and quickly stuck in such a way that the carotid is severed, stopping the flow of blood to the brain, without puncturing the lung cavity, otherwise the blood would spill into it and not reach the heart, which has to keep on beating and pumping to the last drop of blood. This and a diagram was all we had to go by.

So we decided to go ahead on the day of the first full cold moon. Our first pig was positively huge, fed on green apples and buckets of cranberries.... He was Yvonne's friend, and everybody knows it is easier to kill an enemy than a friend. Our argument was, let's face it, we eat meat: animals are usually killed by proxy and then eaten by hypocrites who faint at the sight of blood. Anyone who eats meat is an accessory to the assassination, and if there is one thing I don't like to be, it is an accessory.

We devised a system by which we brought our candid candidate under a block and tackle hanging from a beam. There we gave him a green apple to distract him, the equivalent of a Judas' kiss or the last cigarette. Then I swiftly slipped a double-noosed rope around his hind legs. We discreetly lowered the block and tackle and slipped the rope onto the hook.

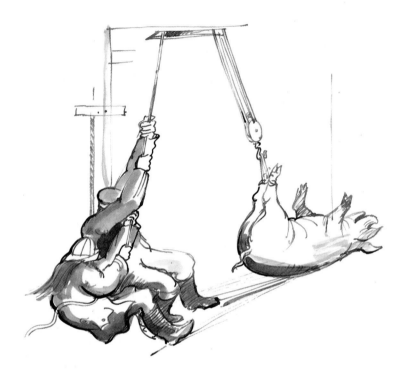

Then we jumped for the rope, and 'hop'! Like bell-ringers tolling tocsins we hoisted the pig into mid-air. Mr Dennis he 'don't' like it at all, and he squeals as if he were on the telly, sponsored by Geritol, hosted by Lawrence Welk . . . .

We had to act fast. Me, knife in one hand, holding one foreleg with the other, Yvonne holding the bucket and the pig by one ear; I plunged in the blade. I tried to follow the diagram and it worked: a jet of blood shot into the bucket, testifying to the success of our intervention. I know now how cosmic it feels to perform such a rite, but I shall never find the words to describe it. And it is just as well: adequate words would only vulgarize the experience. The will-power used for this performance gave us pride and glory.

Yvonne says: 'Man kills either for survival or for vanity.' When we kill, it is for both reasons, if the culinary aspect is to be classified in the survival category. With better food you *do* achieve a better kind of survival. As for vanity: I wouldn't be writing all this if we were not proud of our feats of butchering.

Then we turned the place into a funeral parlor and proceeded to the toilet of the deceased . . . .

We have been told that this was a barbarous way of killing a pig and that it should be stunned beforehand. That point is still being argued. For my apology I shall reproduce here a passage from the pamphlet published by the Morton Salt Co. in the U.S.A.:

'Sticking is the only and most practical, efficient method to kill a pig and also the most humane. It is best not to stun or shoot a hog before sticking, for a good bleed is difficult to obtain when the hogs are stunned.'

One thing we cán vouch for: never had we tasted such good meat, whether fresh, salted, brined, or smoked.

Yvonne cleaned the intestines and we proceeded to fill them up with our mixture for *boudin Alsatien* (Alsatian blood pudding).

We laughed ourselves sick when the bowel being stuffed started to spin and kick like a live eel in season! The whole kitchen was splashed with blood.

The boudin was deliriously delicious.

We went to bed exhausted.

I dreamt that I was one half of the carcass and Yvonne the other half and that we matched each other perfectly. She didn't sleep so well. She dreamt that the in-

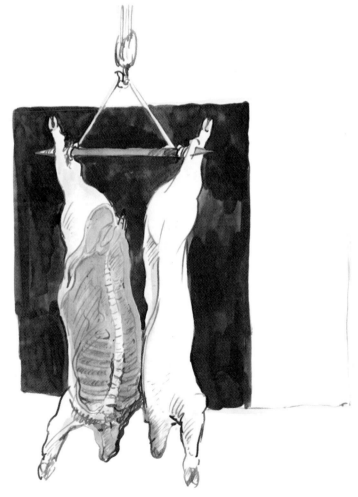

testines and innards were performing some kind of ritual belly-dance around our bed.

The next morning I looked at myself in the mirror and for once found myself rather dashing. It was still full moon, and the full moon fills me with all kinds of brittle sensations. Then I dashed down to the barn. The cold had seized the carcass, which was now ready to be cut.

La victoire en chantant . . . feeling like Bonaparte crowning himself Napoleon, like Bluebeard in front of some new closets . . . . It was another busy day, cutting, trimming, tying and boning, with Yvonne boiling the bones and then scraping them for the *rillettes*.

We leased out the head to Mrs McFlaw who turned it into 'headcheese' for us and our neighbors . . . .

Smokehouse

Life here is punctuated by storms. They hit you when you don't expect them, and it always seems that the last one was the worst. We just had one, two days after the opening of the lobster season. A catastrophe. Funereal fishermen wander along the shore, like lost souls along the black waters of the Styx, picking up whatever dismantled trap the surf deigns to relinquish. It takes a fisherman half a day's work to build a lobster trap; then they are tagged for identification. Well that's it! The season just started, and it is over, overnight. Keene lost 250 traps, equivalent to 125 days of labor, not counting the buoys and the rope.

No wonder that the fisherman's mentality is fatalistic. We ourselves lost half our dunes on the southerly beach. The wind is down; big ten-foot waves furl and uncurl in orderly rows to crash like a foaming kamikaze, eroding the shore line.

I stand there on the beach taking in the ravages. All of the Island fences are gone. Irony of ironies, one wave washes up at my feet a sign I had posted: 'No trespass. No hunting'.

The culvert leading from the pond is blocked with piles of rocks, and the pond is ready to overflow and wash away the thin stretch of land on which our driveway runs.

Called my friend Slam, (the one who gave me the anvil). He owns a fleet of trucks and bulldozers. I'll trade him my tractor for enough rocks to reinforce the northerly shore, otherwise we will end up on an island . . . .

Along the shore scores of dead dovekies, seabirds which live on plankton. When the storms are too fierce and prolonged they cannot manage to feed, and die of starvation.

Stones washed in by the storm have to be picked off the driveway. Bending down under the rushing clouds, I feel them rolling over my back (the clouds, not the stones). A north wind peppered with ice flakes is pecking at my face; tear-bleary eyes.

To slog away like that one has to expend a lot of energy, yet for me it seems to be the opposite: the harder you work, the more energy flows into you. And the closer you feel to the ground, the closer you feel to the sky.

Potatoes?

Canada goose, cruising speed 60 m.ph.

The hunting season has started.... This is one of the biggest events of the year for the masculine segment of this population. Parents will even let their boys skip school in order to go 'ducking' or deer hunting. There is an electric mood of truancy in the air.

Men go in gangs, with ample supplies of liquor and ammunition, to some camp they keep in the woods. A camp is usually a cabin or shack with a stove and some mattresses.

Yvonne and I became fully aware of how dangerous it could be to go into the woods during the hunting season, especially before Christmas, when there is a rush for venison. We were in search of a nice Christmas tree on a wooded piece of property we used to own twenty-five miles away. There we were, when gun shots started puncturing the silence all around us. It was the first time in my life that I have felt 'hunted', and I still have nightmares about it. Then through the thickets of low spruce trees the hunters emerged, with guns of military caliber muzzling in our direction, the men with eyes as red as their jackets, tottering, reeling drunk, not having quite decided whether we were game or not.

I understand now why it is advisable to wear bright colors at this time of the year.

These fishing shacks are now all gone – ducking hunters stripped and burned them to fuel their own camp fires.

Shooting incidents as well as accidents are part of the hunting routine.

'Ed, what happened to your dog?'

'I shot it . . . .'

'Shot it?'

'Yep, I took him for a deer.' Ed had asked me to come along to his camp, but I was too busy with work . . . .

Ed tells me how he was stalking the woods when he heard a strange weeping sound, and came upon a hunter and his wife. The man had just shot a deer. The wife was on her knees holding the head of the deer in her lap, stroking it and sobbing away: 'You poor thing, what have they done to you, never again, never . . . .' The husband standing there, dumbfounded, scratching his neck.

It is not only dogs who get shot. I was told the story of a man who, like us, took a stroll in the woods and was suddenly faced with gunfire. He didn't want to be mistaken for a deer, so he climbed up a tree. He was spotted and mistaken for a bear. The boys had a bit of shooting practice before they had him down – dead. The story in itself would be rather banal if one particular bullet had not, all by itself, made six holes in the sieved body of the victim, 'two holes by going through the right arm, two holes in and out of the chest, and again two holes through the left arm, and that makes six holes altogether, right?'

'Right. *Le compte y est.*'

This is a hunters' paradise as long as the hunters are not hunting each other.

Then again, not all hunters get drunk and restless. But it is always the exceptions that provide the better stories.

The problem presented by hunters seems to affect the whole province. In another locality a woman who lives alone in a house by the woods went to the police to complain that her life was in danger, with all the shooting around her place. She was advised to go and live somewhere else!....

The hunting season does have some magnificent culinary side effects though, like a splendid morsel of moose meat given to us by a neighbor. Cooked it with chanterelles and a little dabble-sauce, *moitié chasseur, moitie Bordelaise, peut-être même Bourguignonne*!

Then some hammed Brussels sprouts, and some salsify tortured in butter. Started on one of Yvonne's fruitcakes, made a year ago. It was kept wrapped in a towel soaked with whisky.

Moose

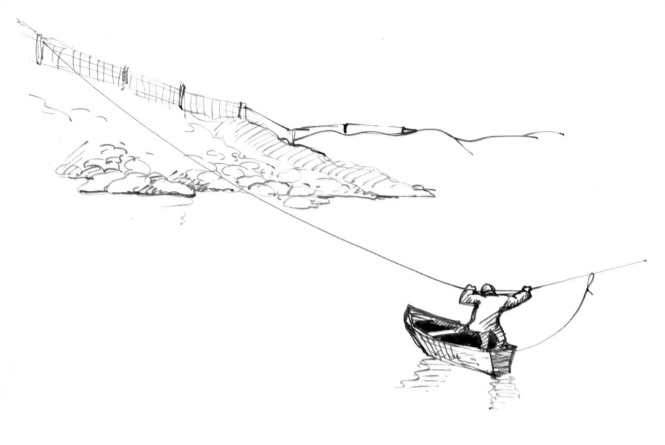

My publisher, Daniel Keel, was visiting me when some blokes landed in a little
boat to have a shot at our ducks in the pond. There was only one way to settle the
matter. Guns can talk. The Remington Yvonne gave me for my birthday is con-
vincingly voluble, and its high velocity bullets have a nice buzzing sound.

So I started shooting at the boys (meaning: over their heads), who ran back to
their boat; I followed them along the shore.

Their outboard engine conked out and they had to row back to land.

One of them pulled out a bottle of rum. We had a few drinks together and
emptied the bottle, which we then took and smashed on a rock, the way the
Russians smash their glasses after emptying them. We have been on good terms
ever since. Through shooting bluff I was respected. (In this case of course I was at
an advantage, since they only had shotguns and I had the real thing.)

One Christmas always brings back memories of others. Our first Christmas here was quite a riot. The new section of the house was roofed and finished but for the shingling. I had already moved our belongings in from storage, including 280 cardboard boxes of books. Then, just at the beginning of our Christmas dinner, a sudden southerly rain storm literally 'blew up', rushing masses of water against the house. The wind drove the rain squirting through the finest cracks, even nail holes. I can truthfully say that the southerly wall was actually spitting at us. So we started to caulk the house with pieces of wood, matchsticks, toilet paper, to no avail. Then we went back to the basement, rearranged the boxes on top of and under sheets of plastic. When we came back to start our dinner, a filet mignon, the dish was empty. There by the table sat Sacha, our Newfoundland dog, his gaping mouth plugged by the roast, which was sticking out like an oversize cigar. Sacha had simply tried to swallow it whole. We pulled it out, gave him the soiled part, and ate the rest.

to be or not to be !

Sacha loves to run after balls. His favorite one is a big round metal floating ball which is too big to fit in his mouth, so that there is no real way for him ever to get hold of it.

The ice on the pond is melting. One of our little games is to send the ball over the thin ice of the pond, and big Sacha runs after it till the ice around him starts to crack, a very special ominous sound of breakage which perfectly fits the situation and Sacha's hysterial barking. So then: the dog's frantic hesitation between his beloved ball or safety on terra firma. We have our laughs when the ice floor finally collapses and Sacha performs a dunce's dance from floe to floe.

Icy waters do not affect him. His breed is made for this kind of trial, from which he emerges ornamented with merrily tinkling icicles hanging from his hair.

Stitch told me that somebody here cut off his dog's tail because the poor beast wagged it every time the mother-in-law came for a visit. A good thing the dog didn't get erections . . . .

Going out to pick up the mail; I found myself accosted by Stan Stumble: 'Hello Mr Ungerer, you see me, yes, you see me right here in front of you, well, don't worry, the doctor gives me one year to live if I go on like this. I am through, I am finished. You, you are a nice man and you can understand, well, I'll tell you I'll drink myself to death for every single day that's left.'

He fondly pats the bottle bulging in his jacket, as if it were a pet of some kind. Then he goes on: 'I just feel terrible about it, my wife, my kids, you understand, you do, just drinking away and making everybody suffer on my account. So long now, so long, I knew you would understand', and he walks off in a tight, busy gait, as if on a call of duty. Then he stops and comes back to me: 'My mother, you know, she thinks the world of you and I know you understand.' Then off again, shuffling, efficiently desperate in search of nothing.

I was informed that last night Crispy came out from a ditch where he was hiding and that he pulled a knife on a girl walking by. 'It's the hot rod or the cold steel' he said . . . . She just swung her handbag and told him to get out of her way. Too much television.

The first time I heard about Crispy was when one of his younger brothers came to warn us that he was planning to kidnap (kitnap) our cats for ransom. He never went ahead with this plan but came to visit us instead, actually to sell us some fish. A small, wiry, spidery, washed-out, threadbare young man. His wife had run out on him and left him with his little girl, age three.

I ask him in, we have a beer . . . .

'I like to fish, on the sea you don't think . . . . Well if I think, it's of my little girl, only thing I got in this world, now look at me, you wouldn't think by looking at me that anybody would like me . . . . But I have one friend, Joy, ugly too.'

'Who's Joy?'

'Joy is It.'

'What do you mean by It?'

'It is an it, not a he, not a she, aw! Ye know what I mean.'

'Oh, you mean homosexual!'

'No, no way, it is an It, that's it.'

'How is that?'

'Let's put it that way, upstairs it looks like a she, downstairs it looks like a he, if you ask me, personally, I'd say it likes girls better.'

'How do you know?'

'Well I know it for a fact . . . .' He looks out of the kitchen window. 'Should be on my way now.'

Es war ein König in Thule

I have finished a book and will take it to Zurich myself. Stitch and his wife will be staying in our house. Before leaving for Europe I have finished smoking our bacons and hams. Stitch comes by as I am hanging them on the ceiling of the barn, shakes his head and says:

'Providin' you and Yevohn come back at all, do you think you can eat all that?'

'Well, Stitch, I guess I'll call my lawyer and put them in my will.'

On the way to the airport we stop at an antique shop in Spillwater.

The owner: 'Where you from?'

'Gull Harbor.'

'Gull Harbor! If I ever saw and made a dollar bill out of Gull Harbor, I'd wash it and hang it on the line.'

Gave him one and told him to go to work, but wash his hands first . . . .

His face turned sour, and his eyes curdled.

Ever since we first arrived, the frequency of fires around here was what struck us the most. Last year one of the town's fisheries burned down. It will remain a spectacle equal to anything I saw during the Second World War. From fire to blaze. They couldn't get the fire truck started. It turned out later that someone had siphoned the gasoline out of the tank.

Small things first, the house of the fishery owner had already been reduced to ashes.

The firemen are volunteers, and so are the fires, it seems.

The houses here are built of wood; they burn well and fast, leaving a black square, in the middle of which stand the fridge, the oven and the tub.

Statistics: arson in Canada is up three hundred per cent. After a while one gets to feel pyronoid about it. When we go to Newbridge to watch what they call a 'fillim' I pack my works in progress, my passport, and my valuables in a suitcase. So there we are going to the movies with luggage the way others go on a vacation or a deportation.

And then we come back we always say with a sigh of relief: 'Look, the house is still there!'

noch steht es da, das alte Haus...

During our absence a conflagration destroyed the centre of town. Here is an excerpt from a letter which reached us:

'Monday night a fire started and half the business section of the town burnt down. Five buildings, two dwellings. Eight families burnt out, no one hurt or dead, thank goodness. It was an awful night. The weather was below zero with a north-west wind of about thirty miles in gusts, and some of us honestly thought the whole town, or at least the whole hill down to our street would go. There were fire engines here from four neighboring municipalities. They all ran out of water, three of them were out of gas and their pumps wouldn't pump.'

Coming home, home. Our friend Brick, who owns a garage and sells second-hand cars is on hand to pick us up. (The airport is 140 miles away . . . .) His car was blight red, the last coat, or rather mantle, of paint having been applied with a roller. Wallpaper would have been more to my taste.

To this day we do not know how we got from there to here. The road was solid ice. The transmission oil started leaking away; the suspension was so soft it felt like we were being driven inside a rotten watermelon. It was getting dark when the lights decided to dim and carry on like some scatter-brained strobe light.

So we had plenty of time to hear the news, again, about the fire, and the gossip as to how and why it started. On top of that the other fishery had gone bankrupt, leaving only one fish plant in operation.

Brick is a volunteer in the local fire department. It was pretty spine-chilling to hear him tell of the fight they put up against a fire in minus-ten-degree weather – the water literally freezing as it came out of the hose, with visions of helpless firemen throwing icicles at the fire!

As we reached the road to our driveway we had to walk the last stretch, Yvonne and I holding on to each other, crashing and skidding on peels of laughter. Tiger, our pet lamb, was the first to spot us and welcome us. We passed by the vegetable

Tiger!

garden, where our big heads of green lettuce were comfortably fending off the winter under their protective frames of plastic and ice.

Home again, Stitch and his wife beaming. I brought Stitch a pocket watch. He stands there holding it in the palm of his big woodsman's hands.

'It's a good one, a good one.'

'How can you tell?'

'By the weight of it.'

What is the news?... well the tenant of the house next door to theirs disappeared. The dog locked inside starved to death.

'Now isn't that something!'

And Kevin's cabin burned down, but that's hardly news since it has already burned down twice. They are in the habit of cutting up old automobile tires and using the stuff as fuel in their stove. The rubber melts and spills over the floor.

Tongue twister: say ten times quickly: Can Kevin's cabin cave in?

Street corner

Gull Harbor has turned into a ghost town. I hear that another fishery down the coast has burned down, a three-million-dollar fire. The teller at the bank says: 'That should help us a bit.'

There is a bit of traverse thinking there, but in fact it means that more boats will be unloading their fish here in the last local fishery still operating.

During the fire my friend Lex, a teacher took his family to some friends' house and went back on to the roof of his own house, performing a kind of mechanical tap dance to step on the inflying sparks. Meanwhile, their friends' little girl kept on asking again and again: 'Do you think Lex has burned by now?' Just the kind of remark the script needed to improve the suspense.... Lex's wife is a teacher as well; they tell us of a family where there's only one dress for two girls, they have to take turns wearing it.... Of a child of another poor family who is dirty and smells so bad no other child would come near her. The other children nicknamed the girl 'plague woman'; they draw hex-signs in the palms of their hands to ward her off. This is about the same as the way the adults here treat a one-eyed man. To be one-eyed here is considered 'evil eye'.

A few years back we invited Lex for dinner. He came across the beach in his Volvo; we had no road then. He had his dinner and drove off as it was getting dark, but a few minutes later he was back, having left his car bogged in the sand already wet from the incoming tide. So we rushed down to the beach with our Land Rover and ropes. It was too late. The tide was in and waves were already tossing the car. Its lights were on. So we quickly called Brick, who came with his tow truck. By then the car was afloat and leisurely drifting away. A good thing Lex had left the lights on, which by now were mischievously blinking. Brick and I went with clothes and all into the icy water to hook the truck's cable onto the car. This we managed, and the Volvo was hauled back to shore, as good as new. The inside was absolutely dry. How about that for a commercial? Only the side of one front door had been stove in by a wave.

Speaking of blinking lights, we were startled one night by the dog barking. Went to the window, and strangely, down at the tip of the beach there was a light sending out signals. The intervals did not fit any code as far as I could see, so I decided to go down and check the who of the what and why . . . . When I got there, the light flashing on, there was a car. In it was a young couple, very much in love. One of the parking lights obviously had a faulty connection. This could have been the couple's problem as well, since I found the flashing more erratic than rhythmic. Lights and delights. It reminded me of how mechanical life's pleasures can be.

DOG

Snowed in, it's like living on a blank page.

Inside, life is warm in a private, downy way. It is lambing time. The ewes are kept inside the barn. Work in the barn. Build a new passageway and more partitions to give each expecting ewe more privacy. One goose, defying the season, is sitting on the steaming dungpile. She'll end up with hard-boiled goslings.

Shingles are nailed to the barn's plank wall. That means that hundreds of nails are sticking out slightly through the wood on the inside, but not enough for us to bother bending them. They are frosted, since metal conducts the cold. When you turn on the lights at night, all these frosty ice crystals are set to twinkling. What a luxury to have starlit walls!

Outside, a leaden sky: shreds of fog are loitering over the pond. It has got suddenly warmer and we let out the ewes and their lambs for a bit of fresh air . . . . Then, out there crossing over the pond, two dogs . . . .

94

This means trouble. Jump for the gun, run, shoot, miss, the dogs run, Sacha after them. One dog slowed down as he tried to slip through the sheep fencing. I plugged him under the left eye. He is wearing a collar with his name scratched on it, 'Sam'. It's either him or our sheep, I cannot afford any feelings. If I don't kill the dogs, they'll come back.

Dear Mr McTurpin, from whom we bought some of our first sheep, died not long ago. Dogs had come and killed some of his sheep. Running after them, gun in hand, he died of a heart attack. The man lived alone with his sister. He loved sheep, so much that he sounded like them, bleating his words through his nose.

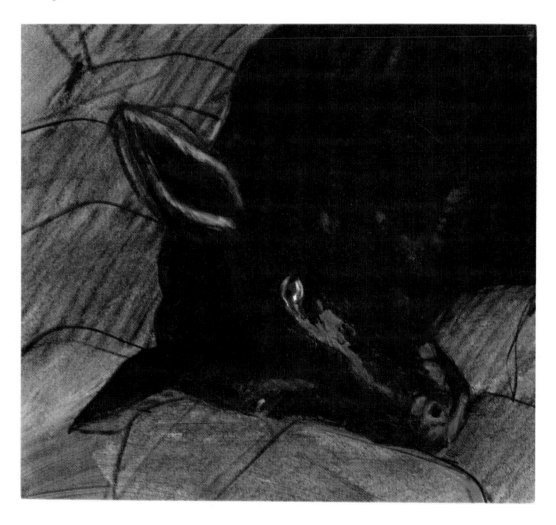

Went to town to shoot some pictures and do a bit of sketching. The weather was grim and sullen. Gull Harbor looked dismal: burnt remnants dissolving in the fog, patches of melting, sulking snow like old laundry ripped off the clotheslines weeks ago. By the docks a kid in a Canadian army jacket was shooting rats.

In a side street came upon half a Volkswagen 'bug'. Yessir, tell me where else in the world would you find *half* a Volkswagen. Someone with a welding torch had very neatly sliced the darling little automobile in two and taken the half with the engine with him, most likely to get it through a door.

The town feels raped. Broken bottles, defaced street signs, the glass panes of the telephone cabin smashed. The wind is leafing through the telephone book.

Credit is available to build a new high school. There is talk of suppressing the teaching of history and geography, since they are not really needed!

By the harbor there is a place which seems to be favored by discarded rubber boots. You can watch them as they lie dying in the ripples of low tide, a necropolis of dead feet. *Cimetière marin* . . . . Yet we like it here, and we like the people as well.

> There is no structure,
> nothing to hang on to,
> nothing to measure your freedom by,
> zero place . . .

Scribbled on a fishing shack:

> Don't close your 👁
> or they'll steal it
> out of your head.

Drugs are definitively moving in.

News item: A 'family man' got himself drunk, grabbed a sledge-hammer, went to the cemetery and smashed 'a few families of tombstones'.

Then an ice storm. Everything is perfectly, systematically, laboriously coated with a thick layer of ice. Lights go out. The electric wires are encased in sausages of ice over an inch in diameter; in places they drag to the ground. You hit the wire with a stick and the ice breaks in a thousand pieces; the wire, relieved, snaps up out of reach.

Walking on the frozen grass: an elephant walking into a baccarat factory wouldn't have a better time. A landscape of shattered chandeliers tinkles under one's feet, *un paysage de lustres à l'envers*.

We went to town to shop and came back. Not only was the house still standing, but we found a beautiful halibut on our doorstep. A present from Strap, most likely.

Strap Tinsel was our first visitor when we moved in, one of our earliest friends and neighbors.

He was about fourteen then, a bit under the weather, drunk. I needed help, especially in cleaning out the pond. The former inhabitants of the place seemed to have dumped all their garbage into this body of water, and this for at least eighty years. It was a sort of sport to go into the water, sometimes waist-deep, searching the muddy bottom and fishing up the most outrageous items. I actually retrieved all the separate components of a gun, which I was able to piece together again.

Strap came from a cluster of houses situated outside the town limits, oddly nicknamed 'Dodge City'. Smashy as well as Fancy come from there. A place turned wild ever since 1961, when eighteen fishermen were lost at sea in one mighty killer storm. Strap and his brothers and little sister Wendy were left fatherless, and the mother took to drink. They are a pretty reckless bunch in Dodge City, but we have always been on good terms with them. One thing I made clear from the beginning: 'If you got drink in you, don't come near here, or I swear I'll shoot you.' That was plain and clear and we were never bothered.

One day Strap plugged one of his brothers with a few mind-soothing bullets.... So I asked him:

'Strap, why did you shoot your brother?'

'Oh, once a year you got to shoot it out.'

His older brother just died, drunk; he gagged on his own vomit. Strap goes fishing on trawlers and we do not see him very often any more.

There used to be a supermarket in town, situated at the bottom of the street leading to the waterfront. That street ends in a T, in the middle of which the said supermarket stood. It was not so super the day the Dodge City boys drove down the street out of control and crashed through its plate-glass window. The car stopped in front of the cash register. No one was hurt. Sorry I wasn't there to see it.

The girl manning the cash register had been elected Queen of Gull Harbor the year we moved to Canada. The committee which organized the First of July festivities (the national holiday) had asked Yvonne to be a judge in this contest. Another jury was to select the mini-queens. This parade is an annual event. Every prospective queen has a sponsor: the bank, the fisheries, and so on. During the parade the girls are officially displayed to the public on floats or spread out on the hoods of cars painstakingly adorned with garlands of paper flowers and strands of colored toilet paper. Majorettes of various ages and origins perform completely out of step with the music, revealing their scantily covered 'in-betweens'. If the girls were more attractive it would be a paedophile's delight, but soft drinks, junk food and sloppy living have uglified even the youngest elements of this 'very modern' society.

There are no bands to speak of. The music blares from speakers out of the yawning trunk of a car. Last year you would have missed the pageant, because it took a wrong turn and suddenly emerged onto the main square, its final destination, while the crowds on Main Street were still eagerly waiting for the procession to show up.

A couple in the next town had adopted a black child. They already had a home-made white son. For their local parade the mother decided to dress up her older boy as a Sicilian organ grinder. Everybody knows that in the old days Sicilian organ grinders always dragged around a little monkey on a leash . . . . Guess who the monkey was?

I had always heard the expression 'a car wrapped around a telephone pole'. Well, we actually saw one. This car had missed a curve and hit a simple, modest, unpretentious little pole. The pole did not break, but the car, an American whale of a thing, had its chassis bent so that the front bumper literally met the rear bumper. That vehicle must have practised yoga for quite a while to be able to accomplish such a feat. The driver, his 'pals' and the telephone pole walked out unharmed.

A sign on an old house:

this property for sale
call me

No name, no telephone number.

A fisherman came to consult my lawyer about his 'testicle' (meaning testament).

A farmer from inland who brought us some cows from an auction: 'Fisherman people, forgive my language, they fish in the summer, in winter they fuck the windows.'

'You mean the widows.'

'No, the windows.'

Flack McGully likes to poach. Everybody knows when he is out on a kill, because he then walks with a stiff leg . . . he hides his gun inside his pants, muzzle down, inside his boot.

Dolly Cunard, forty-five, works with her husband at the fish plant. Yesterday she decided to leave early and asked her husband to drive her home. They stop on the way at the grocery store. The husband comes out of the store with the groceries and finds his wife dead with a bullet in her head. She has just shot herself into another world.

Quote: 'Around here, if people want to take their lives in their hands, more or less, they put a shotgun to their heads. But then you may come out of it still alive with no face.'

Sheep too . . . a ewe may decide to let go and die. It will pick a spot, go on a hunger strike, and fade out.

Our neighbor Broth Archer got himself baptized a Pentecostal because, says his wife, 'His brother Keene, a follower of this faith, has had much more luck in life.'

Two days go by . . . .

'How are things, any better luck lately?'

'Some baptism that was', he mutters, sifting his words through his teeth. 'Couldn't even land me a decent job!'

Blue is considered bad luck. Claudia, a friend of ours from the States, bought a house here and painted it blue.

The neighbor, a grumpy old man, seems upset by the ill choice of colors and warns her of the possible after-effects . . . .

Claudia: 'If blue is bad luck, so how about your eyes, they are blue too, what do you do about that?'

'Me? Had trouble all of my life.'

That's one way of looking at it.

The cormorant: his feathers are not water-repellent, and with wings spread out to dry he looks like an umbrella in a hallway. In an attitude of beatitude, an anchorite bird of pray.

Easter Sunday. A thick fog cocoons the house, effaces contours: I feel caught in the web myself, all is diffuse, like memories. The present hasn't arrived yet. The ice on the pond is trying to melt, it looks like oilcloth: a literary silence reigns. Am I deaf or dumb? The fog erases the smallest sounds.

Easter Monday. Sooty clouds, a landscape transferred to sandpaper: a simple – even humble – day. With calm sadness we discover a ewe that had disappeared. It is dragging a dead lamb between its legs. One leg had got stuck and prevented it being born.

The ewe is worn out. I push part of the lamb back in, unlock the leg and pull on the little cadaver. Yvonne is pulling the ewe in the other direction. From a distance it would seem that, like children, we are fighting over something. 'It's mine!' 'No, it's mine!' Relieved, the sheep runs away as if nothing had happened. Upon us that sweetish smell of pascal maternity.

the end of a dynasty

Went down to the barn to decapitate a rooster. With his head chopped off he still keeps on running. Another rooster, a live one, attacks him; a few seconds later the dead one falls dead on the ground. The triumphant rooster is delighted by his victory and crows apoplectically to publicize his glory. How French!

The sea takes care of everything, the notchless line of the horizon sums down all balance sheets to zero . . . .

The horizon line of the sea is the only sight which to me is graphically and spiritually safe.

My favorite colors are black and white. That is why I like gray the best.

I have this tendency, when working alone, to talk to the objects involved in my activity. I apologize to the tree I am felling, and will blarney a boulder into budging. But I never talk to anything mechanical; I have no audible rapport with the car or my power tools.

Built a new stall in the upper barn. A plank fell down and hit me behind the jaw. Sleepless night with pain and an easterly storm shaking and tossing the house. Life inside a vibrator. There should be a law against weather like that. Easterly storms are the worst for us: the waves come directly from the ocean and crash only sixty feet from the house. Big round stones are propelled by the impact of the waves, and some land not far from our doorstep.

Well, this storm was one of *THEM!* Blind, brutal, merciless and quick. What a mess! It takes weeks to reinforce the shoreline and clean the stones and rubbish off the shore pasture. The parking lot by the house was scooped out. I felt angry, balling my fists against the tides. Yvonne said it served me right, that 'nature must remain a challenge.' So I swallowed my pride with some whisky and picked up my tools.

We had populated the Island with rabbits, but they all disappeared and we found out how. It was a fox, actually so brazen that he'd take his time to sit down by the beach and wait for the tide to pull out. Sacha spotted him, and I started to run after the fox, picking up a stone on the way. The fox ran in a curve, and that enabled Sacha to cut him off. At this point the fox stopped for a fraction of a second, and I threw my stone from a distance of approximately sixty feet. It hit the fox on the side of the head and it fell dead. Now if I had aimed, I'd have never been able to hit anything from such a distance. The fox was dead; as for me, I had to go and see a doctor, since in my rush I had run through some brush and cut the cornea of my eye on a bayberry leaf!

I live in a routine of accidents, and three times now rusty nails have punctured my feet right through the rubber soles of my boots. Like a car, I should be able to keep a spare foot for cases like that. I used that idea in my children's book *The Beast of Monsieur Racine*: in the corner of one of the pictures you can see a tramp with a *croix de guerre* on his chest, carrying a bundle out of which a foot is sticking. Many people, children, parents and white-eyed librarians have asked me what it was doing there. 'Well', I tell them, 'a hobo does a lot of walking and he can use an extra foot.'

Then it snowed again. Noticed that geese eat snow, maybe that is what keeps them so white; geese are so white it seems that detergent is seeping out from the inside. I would call them the nuns of the farmyard if they were not so loud during intercourse.

During the winter we hack open a hole in the frozen pond; geese prefer to mate in the water. This hole turns into a pool of passion whenever the geese decide to lubricate their revels.

They live in flocks and share a communal life. When a goose has sex with her gander the whole establishment makes a circle around the couple to watch, encourage, and scream at them. The din is indescribable. 'Faster!' 'Give it to her!' 'Don't let it out!' etc.... All this usually ends with enthusiastic applause. (They applaud by beating the air with their wings.)

The geese consider that waterhole as *their* property, and will go into fits of vociferating rage when the horses come down to drink *their* water. Only the ducks are fast and clever enough to make fun of them: even at feeding time ducks will crawl between the geese's legs and eat the corn from under their beaks.

Geese are real viragos: they learned to hiss from the snakes. Yet they seem to get along with each other. Much has been written about their social pattern – the discipline, the harmony of precedence in the hierarchy. You can see it when the whole flock goes on a tour of the pond, with ganders on the outside watching for trouble and the mothers framing the nursery of goslings. On terra firma they always keep a male sentry on duty.

Geese are vegetarians and teetotallers. They have strict morals; their cleanliness is a matter of pride. They do not take the name of the Lord in vain.

A politburo makes all the important decisions. They all have social security. Well, not really all. When I say all, I mean the majority of our white geese. The few gray ones are ostracized and enjoy none of the communal benefits.

For instance: on nights when the temperature dips below zero, the white geese stick to each other to keep warm, but the gray ones are not allowed to share this system of central heating. When a goose dies frozen, it is always a gray one.

They have nothing in common with the omnivorous, lawless, raunchy ducks. One look at a cluster of drakes gangraping any old duck will give you an idea of their moral vacuum. Ducks live like gypsies, with no home base. Mother ducks lose most of their ducklings and couldn't care less; on the contrary, I suspect they try to lose them as fast as possible. Ducks have a great waddling sense of rhythm: they run a discothèque, which is much frowned upon by the geese, who, incidentally, have joined the local Baptists and were all baptised by immersion, just like submarines. I say this ironically because the Baptists, clad in white, perform their dipping rites at the end of our beach, and from a distance they do look like a flock of geese. I do not know if baptism in salt water is quite as valid as in fresh water . . . .

Sometimes two geese decide to nest next to each other. Their ganders stand by in the vicinity. Should one goose step outside for a little wash you will observe the neighbor goose slip her eggs under her own wings to keep them warm and then return them when the original owner comes back. This does not always work out so well; occasional confusion may ensure, and endless litigation takes place.

Geese are punctual. Should you be late in the morning at feeding time they will come all the way to the house and raise Cain.

Geese are for me a visual delight.

In the snow especially, a study of competing whitenesses.

I know of no animals with eyes of such piercing blue as the geese's. All their distrust is pinpointed in these glass-bead eyes.

Sometimes when their heads are profiled against a sky of matching blue, you have the impression of looking right through their heads . . . .

They put orange make-up on their beaks.

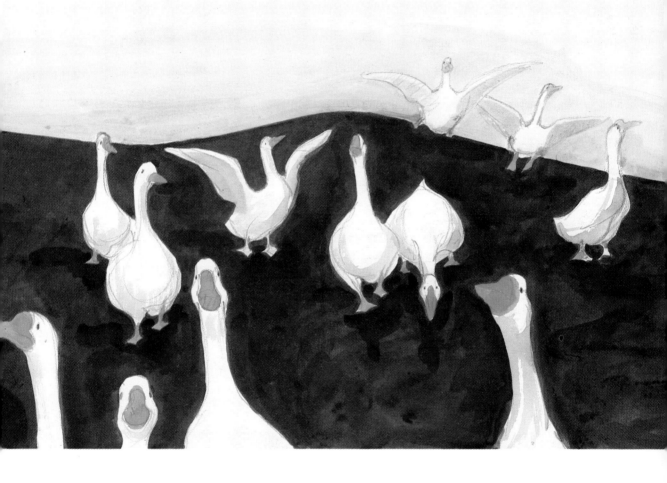

Belted Kingfisher .. un rigolo!

It is impressive to watch a flock of well-fed geese take off, and somewhat comical to see them land, especially on the ice of the pond. Their long necks are stretched like a Concorde's; I can fancy the pilot in command cockpitted behind the beak, the passengers seatbelted inside the goose. It is an incredible spectacle to watch a squadron of these birds crash-landing on the thin mirror of new ice, in a splash among splinters of ice. Later, when the ice has frozen solid, they land and skid out of control on their well-padded behinds.

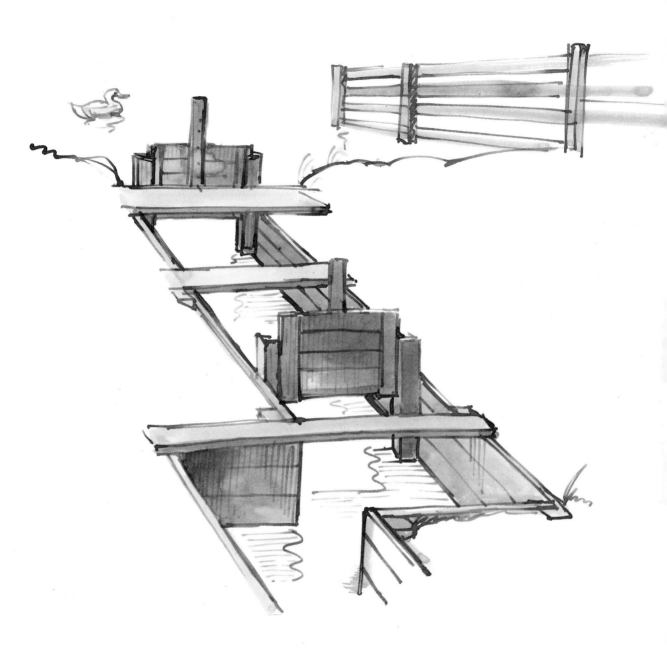

The emergence of spring brings about an emergency of work. Building, fixing, docking the lambs' tails, rebuilding the culvert and sluices . . . . I like the French word *écluse* much better, the word trickles much more into my ears. *Schleuse,* in German sounds rather intestinal, while 'sluice' rhymes too closely with 'juice'.

english soldiers on duty

May the first. Spring has already established a bridgehead on this place, and dispatched delegations of prudish Quaker ladies and innocent-looking patches of blue-eyed grass. Violets, with false modesty, are paving the way for the more garish irises. Erect daffodils are nodding their mouthpieces like old-fashioned telephones.

Birch trees have decided to keep their long winter underwear for the rest of the year. Older trees, in an attempt at spring cleaning, are trying to scratch off mosses and 'Old Man's Beard'. On some rocks redcoated 'British soldiers' have been posted.

Dandelions button the lawn to the ground. They are already planning a take-over of the umbrella and parachute industries, in total defiance of the new anti-trust laws.

Ferns unwind out of hibernation like hair-curlers. In the woods, twinflowers emerge, mated for life. Anemones, pipsissewas and their like seek refuge in anonymity, and I shall not intrude upon their privacy any longer, despite the fact that flowers, like women, like to be noticed and honeyed.

The birches were right to hold on to their flannels. A sudden snowstorm takes us by surprise, irascible winds sweep the area; seas are sudsing up a laundry, and the wind is grinding the top of the waves. One goose, which had established a nest in a very open space, had little goslings this morning. Now she is blown away; the goslings roll on the ground like little yellow balls of wool. Yvonne and I run after them and manage to save two. We bring them back home and install them for the moment in our tub. They became Yvonne's pet geese.

First steps...

One of them simply couldn't learn how to walk; its legs just insisted on going their own separate ways. So we tied the two legs together with a thin rubber band, and how it worked! Literally propelled by the elasticity of the motion, the gosling could hardly stop. It got the idea and was soon walking without its artificial muscle.

The snow was followed by rain. It came down in sheets, in blades slicing the landscape.

Then from calamity to a sudden calm.... The brook is gargling mockingly. The weather clears in time for us to watch a big fat golden sun sink like a doubloon through a slot in our piggy-bank hill behind the pond.

Sleepless night. It is full moon and a storm is spanking the house; life inside a spanking.

Then morning. With the moon still shining and the sun rising, I discover myself with two shadows, a cold one and a warm one. I suddenly fly into a rage at the sight of some crows raiding one of our ducks' nests. Crows love eggs. I grab my twenty-two, not checking the safety catch. Bang! it goes off, shooting a bullet between my feet and making a hole in the floor.

I really shouldn't feel so reckless about crows, since we have one living with us in the house. It was given to us as a present when it was little.

The crow's name is Merlin. He established his residence in the kitchen on top of the refrigerator. He also favors a spot in the living-room on top of the corner cupboard. Commuting from one settlement to the other, his trajectory crosses over the sofa. Most visitors do not know that a crow lives with us. I do not know how many candidates for heart-attacks have paled and screeched in the middle of a conversation when the crow came swooping down, like a phantom umbrella, under their very noses . . . .

This crow's preferred victim is Sacha. Especially when the dog is given a nice meaty bone.

Newfoundland dogs are very big and very clumsy. When they lie down they do not seem to be able to fit their hind legs anywhere, and there is usually one leg stretched out with the inside of its paw facing up. Merlin would pace around the gnawing dog, surveying the layout, and finally stop in front of this paw and zing! sink his beak into its very core.

Sacha jumps up with a howl of pain and hides under the kitchen table, leaving his bone to Merlin, who in the most matter-of-fact way takes possession of his loot. (We later had to get rid of him, explaining to him that, after all, he was born free, and free to go and join his equals.)

Sacha has a hard time fending for himself in this vale of tears. He weighs about a hundred fifty pounds now, the size of a small bear. When he sits on top of a rock he looks sadly regal, yet he is the stooge of this place.

He was born a coward, and all the other animals make fun of him. The goats sent him flying with horned uppercuts, the horses bite him. The worst happens when he is cornered by a congregation of geese, who nip at his hair. And all Heidsieck the cat has to do is stare at him with his yellow laser eyes, and the dog deflates into a hapless mass of black hair. He reminds us of the lion in *The Wizard of Oz*. We once saw him try to sniff a rabbit, which just turned around and with its hind paw sloshed Sacha's big truffle. If Sacha goes near the other animals it is simply because he is maniacally jealous. Any attention given to other animals sends him into fits of rage. He goes into hysterics when Yvonne milks the goats, and desperately tries to snatch some of the food given to the other animals. We have even seen him chew hay and swallow chicken feed and oats and rabbit pellets with a grimace!

Out on the deck we heard Sacha barking in a panic . . . and there was Sundance eating his dog food. Poor Sundance is a terminally sick horse . . . . We try to tell Sacha not to get upset since very soon we will have to take Sundance to the dog food factory, and that – who knows? – being ground to bits and put into cans he might end up in this very bowl . . . . Yvonne was getting a chicken ready for lunch; we went back into the house, the chicken was gone, eloped with Heidsieck, who was already nibbling at it.

Everybody eats everybody else's food around here . . . .

Sacha vents his frustrations on lady visitors, Piper, and himself. He favors elderly ladies, especially ones in white summer dresses. His demonstrative urge surges from his sexual obsessions. The outcome of his dogged embraces is rather messy.

There is one being who seems to favor and endure Sacha's libidinous onslaughts, and that is Piper. Wedged between Sacha's front legs, his head half submerged in the dog's drooling mandibles, the cat masochistically enjoys the ordeal, as high above him the dog spasmodically rocks up a slobbering storm of depravity.

Sacha is faithful to his habits. Every afternoon around five he is beset by a throbbing sexual *Drang* which he soothes with a busy tongue. This tongue is speckled black, like used blotting paper. We try to remonstrate with him: 'Sacha, your tongue is turning black, acidulated from all that sinning! If you go on like that it will soon fall off . . . . Sacha stop it!'

All vices and aberrations are personified by the billy goat, Belzébuth. He stinks and looks the part. In a constant state of excitement he sprays himself with his scented urine, which he squirts about with what looks like a cross between a Mont Blanc fountain pen and a screwdriver! For him this is a question of glamor, of sex appeal.

The goats are about to lamb. I am not kidding when I say that, since one of our ewes had a set of weird-looking lambs. One died, and the other one survived for a while till some dogs killed it, as if to erase a mistake. The finger of guilt pointed at the billy goat, who had satisfied his twisted instincts at the expense of a notably innocent and naive ewe. The result was nothing monstrous, on the contrary, a cute little animal with a kid's face and a lamb's fleece. His name was 'Mufti'. A shoat or a geep.

Stitch, our local encyclopedia, informs me that the same thing happens around here between cats and rabbits. The offspring are called 'cabbits'.

I must admit that sometimes we are instrumental in the performance of certain deviations....

Solid white Mrs Pudding is mother of mothers of all our rabbits. She is dead now, and I am sure that she wouldn't mind my telling this story. She once gave birth to a beautiful black buck. We kept him for breeding purposes. The day came for him to be initiated, sex-wise, and who would be the most understanding, the most receptive person to enlighten his manly wits? Who? His mother, of course!

So we threw him into his mother's cage. He ran amok for a while, and finally did what he was expected to do. Having run around so fast he must have lost his sense of orientation, anyway, he did it all wrong, confusing his mama's face with her genitally more appropriate hind quarters. We named him 'black mother fucker'.

This inevitably leads me to the subject of local weddings.

A wedding reception is usually given in the school gym. A long table is set up on trestles, upon which are displayed all the presents given to the bride and groom. Every present is labelled with the name of the donor, and sometimes the price tag. This is a very effective way of putting cheapskates to shame and of spurring the generosity of your family and friends. On a podium there is another table set for the couple and the self-ordained representative of God.

After voicing a deeply-felt prayer, the couple and the preacher sit at the table, in full view of the crowd, which sits down on benches. Everybody has been equipped with a paper cup filled with Kool-Aid. This beverage is then washed down, after a toast to the couple has been enunciated. Then you are handed a styrofoam plate on which you will find half a sterilized little sandwich and a slice of cake, both sealed in cellophane. The festivities do not last long; neither do the marriages.

Yvonne went to the supermarket and bought a cauliflower. Another woman customer looked at it with a nose wrinkling with suspicion. 'My, you must be one of thems gourmettes!'

Gourmette is evidently the feminine counterpart of 'gourmet'. The word, unknown before, was coined by telefission, with a program called 'The Galloping Gourmet'. Only in America will you find gourmets galloping.

Another sight: a fisherman's wife stacking up boxes of 'Frozen Ready-Fried Fishsticks' in her shopping cart. We ourselves found it difficult to buy fresh fish from fishermen.

It is easier for them to unload the whole catch at the fishery, or dump it at sea if the price is not high enough.

The fish here is excellent. Halibut is absolutely in a class by itself; there is plenty of cod, and cod tongues are a local speciality, and, of course, mackerel and herring. We buy fish by the bushel and smoke them. I like to work away gutting and filetting outside by the deck of our house, surrounded by seagulls performing airborne ballets as they try to catch the remnants I throw in the air.

Then the lobsters. One way to catch them (I have never tried it) is to go at low tide and stick your foot into some rock cracks, and wiggle your toe to attract the lobster's attention. When you feel your toe being pinched, pull it slowly out and the crustacean sucker will follow. I have been sworn to that it could be done. The best way to cook lobster is with a clambake, the way the Indians used to do it. (They can't afford to any more, lobster is too expensive for second – if not third-class citizens.) By the way, the local Indians are the Mic-Macs. I don't think I ever saw one, but some still exist. There is one on the way to Yarmouth who lives in a teepee covered with tarpaper.

For a clambake, as most Americans will know, you first of all dig a sizeable hole in the ground and line it with rocks. You keep a fire burning till the rocks have stored all the heat they can take. Then take out the ashes and embers, line the hole with fresh rockweed, dump in the live lobsters, potatoes, more seaweed, clams, mussels and corn. Top it with still more seaweed, seal off the hole with a canvas, put sand or soil on top of it to seal in the heat and the flavor. That's all. One hour later open up the pit. The lobsters don't like it a bit, but you will.

Other delicacies: eelgrass collected at low tide. It grows on the mudflats and is good with a vinaigrette dressing. Then fiddleheads, the top of a fern as it uncurls out of the ground in spring-time.

Nova Scotia is a paradise for berry pickers. Black, blue, rasp and cran. Wild strawberries are patching the back of our dunes.

A botanical rarity grows in the peat bog, the 'bake-apple berry', which makes a jam that does not relate to anything I have ever tasted.

Mussels and soft shell clams are abundant.

On the rocks off shore near the house there grows a breed of mussels which are full of pearls. We put these mussels in a soup on which we nearly broke our teeth. There we were, spitting out pearls like orange pits until we gave up. We gave the soup and its pearls to the pigs, thereby becoming probably the first people ever *really* to cast pearls before swine.

Most locals will not touch mussels, but they adore soft shell clams.

Quote: 'And she had to be taken to the hospital because she ate too many clams. The doctors had to open up her stomach and scoop out the sand . . . .'

I picture little sand beaches lining the littoral of the lady's digestive tract, with tidal pools of gastric juices and scores of clams relaxing . . . .

'Some comical, huh . . . .' Anyway, if clams are sandy you simply immerse them in water with vinegar, and they will disgorge the grit . . . .

Plants growing along the shore in defiance of the inflooding tides stir my admiration as well as my salivary glands: orache, or lamb's quarters, sea rocket, and beach peas with ball bearing pods. Alas, neither the oyster plant, which tastes like oysters, nor the pineapple weed, which tastes of pineapple, are edible.

'My father he lived down your way, he was a deserter from the navy, and up to no good. His neighbor grew the finest vegetables around here, and every morning he would find his patches raided overnight. So he decided to keep watch and he caught my father red-handed. They had a bit of an argument but my father insisted and said that "as long as you'll grow them I'll steal them". And so the matter was settled and we always had the best possible vegetables on our table.'

Back to clear some woods in the company of the goats. In the spring a lot of brush grows back, faster than the seeded grass, and the goats nip off the shoots as fast as they bud.

Stitch comes down. He usually helps me, but not today. He seems very critical of my exertions.

'Them bushes, they'll all grow back in no time . . . (pause) . . . . They'll grow back in no time at all . . . (pause) . . . . Only way to get rid of them is to cut them on the full moon in August!'

'My, Stitch, that's a lot of brush to cut in twenty-four full-mooned hours . . . .'

So!

*Yvonne's working pants
from an amputated pair of jeans...
bucolic eroticism!*

We needed some rags to make scarecrows. So I put up a sign at the post office that I was looking for old clothes. A lot of people called us up, among them a nice lady who offered an old fur coat from the thirties in perfectly good shape, for twenty dollars. I bought it for Yvonne, on whose shoulders it still survives the eighties.

Went to the post office. There was a package for me. All my cheque stubs and receipts returned by the income tax office, packed in an old chocolate box. How sweet.

Then stopped at the house of the lady who had sold Yvonne her fur coat. She had called to tell us that she had baked two pies for us . . . .

Met Sprat Healy, a friend of ours – small, tight, he looks like an undersized bird of prey. We talk about gardening . . . .

Snapper and Dapper are two bachelor brothers. Dapper keeps a vegetable stand and a bit of a grocery store in a wooden shack on the highway. His business has been upset lately by an intrusion of squirrels. They run up and down the shelves, sometimes knocking down valuable goods.

Dapper is there by the cash register. He keeps a loaded twenty-two on hand; sometimes he grabs it and shoots at some of his frolicking pests.

Someone told me they bought a can of beans there and found a bullet in it.

Snapper is an animal freak. He loves animals, radiantly, lavishly, especially ponies. He buys and sells horses. He purchased a stallion which didn't seem to be impressed by his hugging and smooching; as a matter of fact it turned around, hoofed him square in the face, and knocked him out. A good thing Snapper had no teeth left, otherwise he would have lost them all . . . .

Snapper stretched out on the ground: 'Am I dead?'

Dapper: 'Ye can't be dead if y're talking tah me.'

Chipmunks

Horses can show some pretty jagged behaviour. Yvonne's horse, Rajah, is a tough case in point. He has mustang blood in him, a will of his own, and is always distrustingly alert. Yvonne likes the challenge; I don't.

The posts of our fence are planted nine feet apart. They are joined by alternate eighteen-foot boards.

Yvonne once had Rajah tied to one of these boards. I was working some twenty feet away when I dropped a rake to the ground. Rajah, startled, reared, ripped the board off the fence and took off in a gallop, the board dangling between his legs.

Slinky McWire looks like Donald Duck. Skinny, wispy, cross-eyed. He holds his nose up in the air to keep a pair of bottle-bottom glasses in balance. He works hard and drinks even harder trying to make a life worth living. He has a crop of children.

Right now he is a little bit shook up. He was in an automobile accident last week; the driver was killed.

Slinky came by for a little visit. I was in the vegetable garden weeding. In a cautiously curious way he wanted to find out what was growing there. Our garden attracts a lot of attention, since it is planted in raised beds, and around here you only see such ground formations in military cemeteries. This is just as well, considering all the weird stuff we grow there: fennel, salsify, lamb's lettuce, and chervil are exotic beyond understanding. We get our seeds from Europe . . . .

I gave Slinky some fennel to sniff . . . and he suddenly beamed, blushing with real enthusiasm.

'Holy! that smells real good dear.' (Slinky's grammar substitutes 'dear' for commas, periods, and question marks.) 'I should try some in my pipe dear hey do you get high on that stuff dear gosh ye know I just love to get high dear much better than liquor dear now don't get me wrong I don't shoot no needle stuff like that dear just smoke and them pills and ellessdee it hurt ye none dear . . . .'

'Hey Slinky, did you read about that police raid in Chester, they hauled three million dollars of grass.'

'Yeah! ain't it a shame all that Colombian dope up in smoke dear all gone dear . . . it's just too bad!'

We finally bought the equipment for and put in an electric fence, and that stopped the pony. His name should have been Houdini; he would crawl under the water-fence, unlock gates, squeeze through strands of barbed wire: nothing could stop him, and how he would mock us! So we had just let him have the run of the place, punishing him by feeding the horses when he was on the other side of the fence. But now the electricity has done it: he looks really sad, standing there, like an abandoned toy. Well, better sad than dead. Actually he was more of a cute nuisance than anything.

He was interfering with the sheep's feeding one day when, in a fit of annoyance, I took a small stone and threw it at him. I do not know where it hit him, but he collapsed on the ground, his four feet in the air shaking in spasms. That was a horrible moment; I thought I had killed him. I had forgotten about my curse with stones, or whatever you call it. Stones will fly out of my hands and do things. I cannot explain it, but I can feel it. So did the fox.

Summer....

Blades of high beach grass are duelling in the breeze.

Grasshoppers pop and hop: what kind of life is this, never knowing where you will land?....

Jovial, cheeky, well-fed cumuli are leisurely pillowing the blue enameled sky.

Days when you just take it all in....

All round us seagulls are blitzing the rocky shore with saturation bombings. They love sea urchins, mussels, and whelks, but cannot open them. Taking them in their beaks they soar and let them fall on the rocks, where they shatter on impact.

Our house, overlooking the pond and facing the sea, is sandwiched between several ecological zones: the ocean, the shore, the grasslands, the pond, the marsh, the bog, and the woods. Our windows replace television, providing us with a great variety of programs performed by animals with an inborn talent for entertainment, programs sponsored by Aesop, La Fontaine, and Buffon. I am not a naturalist but simply a spectator who collects nature's trivia. I favour plants,

133

Muskrat

animals, and rocks whose originality is enhanced by extremes of color, behaviour, or performance.

Poison hemlock grows in huge clusters around the house, enough to wipe out whole symposia of Socrates. Living in close quarters with it, its modest relative caraway is available to sprinkle seed on Yvonne's bread.

The pond has a population of muskrats paddling about, dragging fresh grass by the mouthful to their underground nests. The entrance to these bunkers is under water and forms a syphon or trap very much like the one adorning the underbellies of our bathroom sinks. Muskrats have definite territories which they survey with the scent of their musk, like women with Givenchy or Chanel.

Great blue herons wade and fish for eels, which cleverly wrap themselves around the birds' beaks, in mytho-laocoonical self-defense.

Osprey

Ospreys, our local grandees, occasionally soar by to dive in splashes, talonning surfacing fish. Like nobility, the osprey is menaced with extinction, since they feed on fish stocked up on DDT, which softens their eggshells.

Bald eagles are rarely seen.

the bluet with bamboostick body

Lady slipper

The fields, woods, and bogs are botanically provocative.

Behind my back, orchids stick out their tongues, fringed by gossip.

In the shade, the lady's slipper waiting for a lady: the lonely, hairless scrotum of the woods.

In the bog, sharing the same flat, three related species of orchid live in a *ménage à trois*. They go by the lovely names of calopogon, arethusa, and pogonia. All three are brazenly pink, except for one botanically rare variety, which is white and innocent.

pogonia   *arethusa*   *calopogon*

pitcher plant.

    The pitcher plant has no interest in baseball whatsoever. Erect amid a cluster of hollow fallopian leaves, it attracts insects which foolishly lose themselves inside these vesicular containers filled with water. There they drown and decompose, giving placid nourishment to the plant.

    Sundew, also carnivorous, has leaves covered with gland-tipped hairs which exude a sticky sweat. It works like flypaper.

    Bon appétit.

painted turtle

By the road we met a painted turtle hitchhiking. We picked her up and invited her to stay with us in the pond. She did and had offspring. Yvonne was dazedozing on the beach in the sun one day when she felt someone scratching her back. She thought it was me sneaking about silently, but no: it was a young painted turtle in full attire. Shocking.

monarch butterfly

The monarch butterfly migrates all the way from South America, flying at an altitude of 600 feet. It feeds on milkweed, which gives it its stink and bad taste. The skunk of butterflies, it survives unharmed. It is a rare and valued butterfly in Europe, since to my knowledge milkweed does not grow there.

Back in the grass, commandos of leopard frogs live in hiding, waiting for D-Day. They wear the same camouflage outfits displayed by French paratroopers, except for the wine-red béret.

Leopard frog.

Bunch berries

Touch me not
(impatiens)

Touch-me-not: its name sounds like a warning. Its pods when ripe will explode at the slightest touch, like a booby-trap, scattering its shrapnel seeds. This plant provides the only known cure for poison ivy: stew it, drain the broth into ice-cube trays, and keep it frozen. In times of need rub an ice cube over the blister-blighted skin.

Since its flower hangs like an earring, the touch-me-not is also known as the jewelweed.

Indian Pipes grow pellucid, wax white, under the spruce trees, with no other vegetal competition: ghostly denizens which, like fungi, feed on decayed matters and shun light. They grow in spectral silence, impervious to chlorophyll, a calumet of peace to the dead Indians' souls.

Indian pipes

Ruby throated humming bird

My taste for records and performance is delighted by two birds:

The ruby-throated hummingbird, a late summer vacationist. Three inches in size, it prides itself on having the best-developed pectoral muscles in the animal kingdom. This minicopter will sustain itself in suspended flight with fifty-five wingbeats a second. In courtship this can rise to 200 wingbeats a second, showing what lubricity can do.

The loon: his dives for fish will take him down 180 feet below sea level; he can remain submerged for fifteen minutes. His nocturnal wailings offshore at night sound like a drowning child, chilling one's ears and curdling one's marrow.

Loon, or great northern diver

goldfinch

Goldfinch: we have a goldmine of these finches, settling like nuggets upon the thistles which barb our grassland.

Red-winged blackbird: is it penis envy that attracts this little cleric to the cattails' phallicity?

*Red wing black bird
with Freudian penis envy*

Flicker!

The flicker: with a red nape, a black mustache matching its black bib, its chest spotted like a Dalmatian dog's, and yellow sprinkled over its wings, this bird has original tastes. He is a woodpecker, feeding mainly on ants. A skilled driller, he has turned one of our electric fence posts into a Swiss cheese to house his family.

The raccoon: this nimble-fingered predator, a cross between Harlequin and Arsène Lupin, will unlock the gates of a chicken coop and neatly wring the fowls' necks. He is reputed to wash his victims before meals, and, as a pet, should be trained to help you with your laundry and the dishes.

Racoon

porcupine

The porcupine: the messy Struwelpeter of our woods. Feeding on bark, he destroys trees for a living. The mother bears one child a year, which is born with ready-made quills. 'They'd better come out pointing in the right direction,' says Yvonne with gonadotropic anxiety.

It is reputed to be edible, but we found the porcupine as distasteful as it looks.

An ice-skating rink was inaugurated in Newbridge. Ice hockey is the national sport, and the youngsters are now able to practise seriously. Talked about it to Stan Gray who was hanging around the liquor shop. He was there for the inaugural match. He is very upset because 'There was niggers in the audience and even some niggers playing!'...'My, thems niggers is not even real people, they should be kept chained outsides.'...

Another sport around here, now falling into disuse, is 'to broom the coon'. You pile up in a car, along with some brooms, and you drive to Newbridge and park somewhere on Main Street. When a Negro comes along you lower the windows and you stick out the brooms and wave them at the hapless passer-by.

Newbridge is an old Loyalist town. At the time of the Declaration of Independence some American families loyal to the King of England left the United States and settled in Canada, taking their slaves along with them.

There is one family of blacks in Gull Harbor. They live marginally. I never had the opportunity to get to know them; it would have been 'fake' and curiosity-driven, and thus offensive on my part to force an acquaintance. I went so far as to take a picture of the head of the family to make a drawing from.

He smiled sadly and said, 'Ahm too dark for your camirah'. I felt very embarrassed, as if I had nosed myself into somebody else's private despair.

(The children of this family turned out very well, and one daughter ran for Canada in the Olympics. Someone did organize a collection in town to help her finance the travelling expenses to Montreal. A miserly forty dollars was the result.)

One last quote to polish off this paragraph:

'I hate them goddam niggers. Of course I only know Tom Brown here in town, and he is all right.'

146

Heidsieck has been in pain lately. We take him to see a vet. The verdict is final: cancer of the bone. The cat has to be put to death.

A friend, depository of so many memories, has left us. There is a gaping hole in the texture of our life.

Heidsieck was a Burmese cat. I had bought him along with Piper, his younger half-brother, in New York for Yvonne when we met.

He was a very proud, class-conscious cat, who would never lower his standards to such menial tasks as hunting. He had the noble presence of a pharaoh's mummy, and looked as if he had just stepped out of a hieroglyph. We should have built a pyramid to his memory.

148

He would refuse to eat unless left in total privacy, though once we fooled him: I had fetched a fairly large piece of plastic pipe, in the middle of which we baited a very special dainty lunch of chopped meat. We placed Heidsieck at one end of the pipe and he crawled in to enjoy his meal in peace. Unbeknownst to him, we introduced Piper at the other end. The pipe suddenly shook and rolled convulsively echoing a duet of screeches. The cats, fighting with arched backs, could not easily back out of the pipe, and we finally had to pull them out by their tails. For once Heidsieck's pride emerged ruffled and tousled and badly in need of loving. He loved affection, and when he got the slightest caress he would literally melt like a piece of butter.

He would never hunt rats, mice, or birds. He made only one exception, for young bunny rabbits. He just could not resist the fun of catching these toy-like hoppers.

There was one very fast and clever survivor who took shelter under the wood-pile, where the cat couldn't reach him. Yvonne named him 'Scooter'. Well, Heidsieck did get him, in front of Yvonne's eyes. She cried and cried.

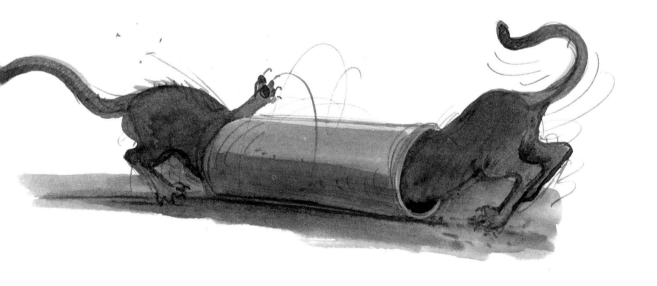

Piper on the other hand, is a reckless rogue, unyielding to any form of affection except the dog's deviate performance already described.

He is a relentless hunter: out all day, out all night. No weather will stop him. He is the only cat I have ever seen fearless of water. Ornithologically, he is devastating. We have a hard time keeping him inside; when we do he punishes us by urinating on the carpets. There was a time when every morning he would step out of the house and come back soon afterwards with a tern. To correct this bad habit we resorted to an old-fashioned trick, which consists in tying a dead bird around the cat's neck. A tern is a rather large bird. Piper carried it around for a whole day. He didn't seem to mind very much, and the following day we let him out, still dragging his victim on the ground. He was back half an hour later with a new victim in his jowls and the old one still tied around his neck. He looked like Josephine Baker at the Folies-Bergères, in a display of feathers.

How Piper is able to catch these birds is a mystery; terns are aggressive. Sickle-winged, they will dive like stukas, aiming for the head of would-be predators. But in contrast to its bellicose behaviour, the tern also stands out for its good manners: in courtship it will present its future partner with a fish, the way humans do with a bouquet of flowers.

Every night we lock up the barn. We take Piper along and drop him there to work on the rats. One night we snuck silently into the barn. We had it all planned. I would drop the cat inside a stall and Yvonne would flick on the light at the same moment. It worked perfectly. The scene that was given to us to witness was performed with wizardry:

Piper catching three rats in one flash. One with each paw, the third with his teeth.

Now that Heidsieck is gone, Piper's personality has changed overnight. He has become loving and lovable, stays home, and doesn't go out hunting any more.

Cats are clever, and they know it. Still, they can be fooled like anybody else. Between the kitchen and the entrace hall we have a glass door, which for a long time had a glass pane missing. The cats were in the habit of using this blank space as a passage. The day a new pane was mounted in its proper place was a day of great pain for our cats. They kept trying to hop through it but would crash against the glass. How we enjoyed their discomfiture, egging them on with cat-calls, sneers and cheers. *En français on peut bien dire qu'ils sont tombés dans le panneau.*

Ridiculed, they seemed to have lost some of their feline cunning.

I tried a similar trick on chickens, spreading grain under an old window. They started pecking at what they saw but couldn't reach, and would have gone on forever; so if you have chickens that seem bored, just keep them busy that way.

I have a weakness for practical jokes. The trouble is, you cannot play them on yourself to find out how it feels.

Captain Beam was still working on our house when we moved in. He is a retired fishing-boat captain and sailmaker by trade as well. He is a Newfy, which means that he comes from Newfoundland. He is a quiet man of enormous stature and heavily-timbered body. He has a heart of warm gold which he keeps hidden under layers of sheer modesty. When he builds a house or a barn he builds it like a ship. (I wish he had built me, especially with a stronger back.)

He and some of the boys had finished plastering a wall. It was on a Friday evening. I planted a few headless nails in that wall and spiked the pointed ends of carrots on them in a row. The carrots sticking out of the wall made a kind of coathanger effect.

The boys returned to work on Monday and did not fail to notice the phenomenon, but they just couldn't get themselves to ask me about it.

I finally took the initiative:

'You have been wondering about my carrots, haven't you?'

'Hm.'

'It's an Old World trick, you dig a hole in the plaster, put in a carrot seed, spackle it shut, water it every now and then . . . .'

'Hm, I be darned . . . .'

The majority of people here are of Scottish descent. They were brought in when the French were scattered from what was then called Acadia. It was one of the first instances in modern history of massive expropriation and deportation, with men forcibly separated from their families. The Scottish newcomers kept some of the local French names, which are pronounced in the most unexpected fashion. Port Mouton, instead of having been renamed Port Mutton, is pronounced Port Motoon.

People here have a hard time showing their feelings. The use of language is rather constipated; the words have a 'hard' time coming out. You'll hardly ever hear someone singing or scattering laughter in the wind. Only 'Eyetalians' do that sort of thing. If something is funny, it is 'some comical', no more, no less. It doesn't mean that people are rank or musty or have no heart; just that it's all kept inside in freezer bags.

Heidsieck's death seems to have inaugurated a string of bad days: a duckling born blind swims in circles. Another one gets caught behind the planking of the culvert; it is impossible to rescue it. Yvonne is beside herself. On the way to fetch the mail in town I rescue another duckling, lost, half-drowned. I take off one of my socks, wrap him up in it, and install him on the seat next to mine. At the post office there is a big package of books from my Swiss publisher, Diogenes Verlag. I drop the package carelessly on the seat. Only at home do I remember the duckling. Crushed and flattened.

When fate says 'now!' it is now! Here today.... I think of an acquaintance of mine. He left New York with his whole family to go and live in Florence so they could stay together with his oldest boy, who had refused to fight in Vietnam. The boy died in a traffic accident. Had he been drafted, would he have died the same day from a bullet?

Away for a few days. Stitch and Sadie stayed at the house. We return, sit down, and what's new....

'Nothing's new, nothing, but for Sunny Logan, he died.'

'Died!'

'Died. Got up in the morning, bent down to put on a sock and collapsed dead. Here today, gone tomorrow.'

We are felled by the news. Sunny dead! 'You are nice to us, we are nice to you'; and now he is gone for good. His passion in life was to find the perfect Christmas tree every year. He would travel around for days till he found perfection. With Sunny dead there will never be another perfect Christmas tree.

Then Sunshine, our second best ewe, died, overnight, just like that. Yvonne had just shorn her. We found her the next morning. A seminary of crows had already gouged her eyes out.

Breakfast: the spout of the coffee pot reminds me of Heidsieck's tail....

From the kitchen table one can see in three different directions. This house has a lot of windows, all divided into small panes, as if segmenting the landscape into that many postcards. Out at sea a boat, or in the sky the clouds, will move from one postcard to another.

Right now a visitor has climbed the deck and looks in through the glass door. It is Tiger. Tiger is not a tiger, but a ewe. She is the daughter of Flitter, our first ewe, who was by nature a bad mother; she tried to kill her lamb after it was born. Yvonne had to take it away from her and bottle-feed it. It was just like nursing a baby. Yvonne had to get up twice every night to feed it. The lamb grew very attached to us and still to this day will respond and run over whenever called by its name: 'Tiger!' This turned out to be very practical: sheep can be very difficult to round up. But whenever we called Tiger the others would follow. When a film crew came to visit us for an interview I made use of an old plastic female bust (the kind used to display sweaters in store windows in Marilyn Monroe's time) by perforating the tip of its breast and introducing the nipples of Tiger's bottles through it to feed him.

Sacha was Tiger's playmate and it was the most heartening sight to watch them frolic and play games like hide-and-seek or King of the Mountain, and Monopoly on rainy days.

Tiger has grown to be a bad mother as well. We were too late when she had her first set of twins. One had already been butted to death; the other we gave for adoption to some homesteading friends. We kept Tiger for love and practicality.

The goats are milked again. Lady gives two quarts a day.

A spell of carpentry, a 'hothouse' for the chickies, two folding sawhorses, for the kitchen a holder for the paper towels, a hutch, and a bench to sit out on the deck.

We drove in the sheep, wormed them, and I pinched the young males. This is one thing I loathe doing. Young sheep have testicles the same size as an adult human's.

The weather is hot, but by the shore we are never pestered by bugs, blackflies or mosquitoes. A thick fog has settled over the area. Summer fogs feel very different from winter fogs, out of place, quaint; one feels out of place, and quaint, oneself.

Filleted and smoked a lot of fish.

One summer Yvonne and I consumed thirty pounds of smoked salmon, in every possible way: on rye bread with cream cheese, onions and lemons, or cut in slivers. You fry it very lightly with thin slices of onion, pour beaten eggs on top of it and scramble the whole thing, a speciality of New York Jewish delicatessens. Or if you have company, put half a smoked salmon in the oven, in a dish with milk and onions.

Sandpipers: like busy little sewing machines on their needle-thin legs they stitch the sandy shore onto the water's edge.

This place has its ups and downs.

The news is that aunt Maggie died. She was Canada's oldest midget, and her brother Sigmund, already dead, had been Canada's smallest denizen ever. Both of them had lived here in town.

Stitch: 'And Sigmund, I knew him well, Sigmund he went into the woods one day to set some snares. He caught a rabbit, but he had to come back to town to get some help, to carry the rabbit, which was too heavy for him. [*Silence*]. To tell you how small he was.' It sounds like a tall story. But Gull Harbor was the home of the smallest dwarf in Canada.

A mute swan landed on our pond, the first one ever seen in the province of Nova Scotia. He must have been caught in a storm, lost his bearings, and diverted here to the nearest emergency landing spot. We alerted the Department of Land and Forests. They sent an investigator to watch over the safety of this *rara avis*. (People here are rather trigger-happy when it comes to shooting at the unusual.)

The sadness emanating from the noble, stranded visitor. The next day he flew away, circled our place once and left, like a prince looking for a fairy tale.

160

This entry marks the end of my diary for 1974-5. That year was the culmination of our stay in Canada. When Yvonne became pregnant we decided to move to Ireland. That was in the early spring of 1976. We came back to Canada to close down the farm. During these two years between old and new roots my father-in-law stayed at the farm all by himself.

The following notes date from our later stays:

Winter '76:

We found one of Yvonne's pet geese dead. Tracks pointed to a wildcat. A gourmet at that, who had carefully managed to cut off its head, and clawed just enough of a hole in the carcass to reach the liver: the rest of the bird was left intact. Two days later another pet goose, same place, same tracks, again only the liver gone.

Wildcats make one mistake: they always follow the same route. I borrowed a trap and set it up in the woods. To my surprise, it caught a beautiful fox. There it was with a crushed leg, looking at me, knowing its time had come. I had to kill it. I left the trap, for a wildcat was the assassin, and the wildcat must go. I got him the next morning, a huge gray beast, again that same haunting expression in his eyes, that knowledge of death . . . . I took it back to Yvonne. I must admit here that I had never seen a real wildcat in my life, but I knew one thing: a wildcat has no tail, and this one had one.

The phone rang two days later; it was a neighbor from up the hill. 'You haven't seen our gray cat lately? It's been gone two days now . . . .'

I didn't have the courage to tell the truth, but we just couldn't feed their cat with our goose liver . . . .

In the meantime Stitch's chicken coop has been raided by a raccoon.

As a last hurrah we kill our last pig, Irma la douce.

I stick her, and pulling out the blade I gash my left middle finger. Our blood mixes. Just then I spot a dog a good hundred yards away, and the sheep are out there! I grab the twenty-two, shoot and hit! I run down across the beach to give it the *coup de grace*. Again this imploring look in its eyes drilling into my killer's guilt. On the way back I come upon a duck agonizing, wounded by hunters, again the same look but rounder, more pinpointed. To stop its suffering I grab a rock and crush its head without looking. Then I jump in the car and drive to the doctor. The office is full of patients, which is not really the word for them. With social security people don't have to pay for medical care, so to go to the doctor's is for many a way to kill time.

Women cackle away along these lines.

'My dear, I was passing gas every five minutes . . . .'

'That's nothing, dearie, I was passing no gas at all an' was bloating somethin' awful and my heart couldn't find space to beat anymore . . . .'

'Well, I had that too of course, but my hands and knees started swelling and I could hardly move and told my husband, Al, something must be done about it . . . .'

No wonder the doctor got fed up with all that and later took up a job cutting fish at the fishery. He was replaced by a doctor who turned out to be a fake and who was tried for criminal negligence. He was well liked and some people wanted him to stay on, diploma or no diploma . . . .

It was announced on the news that this was to be the worst day of the year, seemingly because of some malignment between Saturn and Venus.

For us it was. The dogs came. After all these years we knew that they would come some day . . . .

Ironically, I had just built a new corral to keep the sheep in safety during the night. Ewes lambing were inside the barn . . . .

It went like this:

Yvonne wakes up in the middle of the night and says:

'I hear dogs barking.'

I open a window, yes, dogs are barking. The night is calm and clear, and sounds carry a long way. It wouldn't be on our place, anyway, Sacha would be barking . . . . But a woman's instincts rarely miss, and Yvonne feels uneasy about it. I get dressed and grab the twenty-two, on which I have mounted a flashlight so that at a distance of forty feet the bullet will hit the middle of the circle of light. I go to the barn. Inside all is in order, though the ewes are fidgety . . . . But then the corral, the gate swinging open, in front of it one sheep in agony, her stomach ripped open, her intestines unrolled all over the place, another one disembowelled inside the corral; some survivors are huddled in a mess of blood and torn wool . . . .

The morning after

meat scale

The other sheep are missing.

I still can hear the hysterical yelping of the dogs in the east by the cliffs, driving the survivors over the edge.

I run as fast as one can run; they sense my approach and take flight, led by a little black female from town, red-eyed in the beam of my flashlight. I pull the trigger: click. I had forgotten to load the gun. I scream for ammunition, my father-in-law by now has joined me, it's too late, and it's all over . . . .

And Sacha . . . Sacha joined the gang. After years with sheep, Sacha joined the kill.

We figured out what had happened. The dogs barking around the corral drove the sheep into such a frenzy that they knocked the gate open from the inside . . . .

The next morning, what a mess to clean up.

A few days later: we have one Cheviott ewe with a Jewish nose, her name is Salome. She is very heavy and most certainly will have a set of twins.

We get up at night during the lambing season to see if our assistance is needed.

Salome's water bag has broken, not followed by any cramps. Only eight hours later does she go into labor.

Heaving, pushing, she lies there and nothing happens. It is time for action. I wash my hands and there we go . . . . There is one leg there, I follow it gently, yes and there, the other one, and a third across the way, gently now, slip that one out of the way, so, in the clear. I pull gently on the front paws, then the whole thing blocks. There is another leg coming out of nowhere, which has just unfolded, barring the exit of our little mischief maker . . . .

I push the whole thing back and start all over, again and again, each time something else happens. I am wearing out, we had better call the vet. I take a little rest, then go back to the Chinese puzzle. Salome is panting, her eyes are bulging, so once more up that leg, a front leg, I can feel the head that goes with it, now this leg here, where does it go, nothing. I am overtaken by helplessness and exhaustion; the ewe, exhausted, is giving up and doesn't push anymore . . . a gush of blood out of nowhere gloves my hand in red. The vet from Bridgewater, an hour's drive away, arrives . . . .

Triplets, she has triplets. The vet pulls out one after the other, dead; the mother died later of exhaustion. I feel stupid, criminal, vain.

The dogs' raid and Salome's wretched death marked the end of this part of our lives. We closed the farm down.

The expression on that trapped fox's face still haunts me. Even if I do like to brag about my butchering feats, I was not really cut out for the job. I, who rescue bugs drowning in puddles, and Yvonne, who wouldn't hurt a spider in our house, had been able to overcome our repugnance for killing, but this latest carnage was too much. So now, fed up with the bloody carnival, we moved on . . . .

Postscript:

January 1981: season's greetings from Gull Harbor. 'All is well, we had a wonderful Christmas only someone got into the recreation center and unloaded sixty rounds of ammunition.'

We have kept the house and go back there every summer with our three children. The town seems to be picking up. Fish is selling well, there is a new high school, many houses have been repainted.

Our house, well looked after by friends, is in tiptop shape despite the fact that it was broken into. The arm of the law here is boneless, and the little hoods who were caught got a reprimand while we got the bill for repairs.

The First of July celebrations topped all previous ones. With parade, barbecues, games, displays. A grand dancing soirée was organized, but the band from Halifax never materialized. The celebrators, I imagine, danced *sans musique*, the way they do in silent movies.

We still had a ram left on duty with a sheep-raising friend. Its time to turn into mutton for our summer fare had come. I took the duly dressed carcass to the fishery's cold-storage room. The following Friday at five I picked it up. By five o'clock the next morning the fish plant was gone: it had burned down overnight in a gigantic blaze.

Now, looking back, it seems that our stay coincided with this locality's time-crises, choked between puberty and menopause, adjusting to modern times.

A new fishing plant has been erected, one of the most modern in North America. Bungalows and trailer homes are elbowing out the few remaining old houses.

Economically, the town has been born again, a landmark of mediocrity.

At the tip of our island there is a rock that looks *exactly* like Sacha's head: sniffing the high water mark, staring sadly with geological serenity.